DON'T SHOOT ME...
I'M JUST THE REAL ESTATE AGENT!

DON'T SHOOT ME...
I'M JUST THE REAL ESTATE AGENT!

---

100 Risks for Sellers, Buyers, and Agents

BY

CARI LYNN PACE

authorHOUSE®

AuthorHouse™
1663 Liberty Drive
Bloomington, IN 47403
www.authorhouse.com
Phone: 1-800-839-8640

First published by AuthorHouse 2/19/2010

ISBN: 978-1-4490-8480-6 (e)
ISBN: 978-1-4490-8478-3 (sc)

Library of Congress Control Number: 2010902026

Printed in the United States of America
Bloomington, Indiana

This book is printed on acid-free paper.

Contact Cari Lynn Pace at www.TopRealEstateRisk.com
Or email her at TopRealEstateRisk@gmail.com
Phone (415) 893-9888

DEDICATION

To my husband, Dr. Bob Koch, who willingly served in so many capacities to help me write this book. You have been an encouraging cheerleader, a careful proof reader, my sandwich maker when I (often) got so busy I forgot to eat, and my biggest fan. Thank you for being my life partner!

ACKNOWLEDGEMENTS

My parents, Don and Betty Boyle, always enjoyed hearing of my latest real estate adventures. They told me "You ought to write all this stuff down, Cari!" And so I have.

Many generous professionals lent their enthusiasm and support to my efforts in writing this book. I am lucky to have such friends!

I am also fortunate to have worked with so many talented real estate attorneys throughout the San Francisco Bay Area. Although they hired me for my real estate expertise, I could not help but learn from them. Their wisdom and legal knowledge were the basis for many suggestions offered in this book.

Fellow Realtors® who gave me their valuable and practical input include Clark Rosen and Bruce Wrisley, as well as Kathleen Freitag, Deniz Ince, Fred Angeli, and Kay Moore. I double-checked insurance info with Dennis Hagerty. I thank the well-respected real estate attorney Albert Cordova for his legal review of the points covered in this book.

The amusing cover artwork based on an original watercolor done by Peter F. Maier of San Rafael. I am indebted to Fred Saland for his clever computer mastery to help make this book cover come alive!

The contents of this book easily came together over the years as I taught classes in Risk Management and worked on so many real estate cases. However, the technicalities of getting this book published were new to me and presented many hurdles. I appreciated the advice and guidance of Edward Segal, who has published several of his own books, to help me accomplish this project.

I'd also like to acknowledge the longstanding wisdom and encouragement of my legal mentor, James McKenney, Esq. Jim is a brilliant and much-admired real estate attorney and counsel to *Professional Publishing Plain*

Language™ forms and *TrueForms*™. Over the decades, Jim's generosity with his valuable time and willingness to share his legal expertise has improved our industry. Jim is a blessing to me and those who know him in the real estate community.

Thanks to each of you for your support!

Cari Lynn Pace
March, 2010

Table of Contents

The Finish Line Details

Index to Sidebars:

FOREWORD

This book describes 100 actual examples of real estate transactions which contain "red flags". In real estate jargon, as in life, a red flag is an indicator that there may be potential problems. Agents, Buyers, and Sellers will want to take a good look at the situation and figure out what, if anything, needs to be done. Ignoring a red flag can lead to major troubles. The purpose of this book is to head off any such issues by offering suggestions to Agents, Sellers, and Buyers how they might resolve them.

Each of these real-world situations has been drawn from my 36-plus years as a real estate broker in California. Over the years, I have handled nearly every type of property, both residential and commercial. I've represented Buyers and Sellers of Sausalito houseboats on San Francisco Bay, multiple residences in Lake Tahoe, condominiums in Novato, and exclusive waterfront estates on Belvedere Island. I've also worked for years as a managing broker, supervising Agents for small and large firms. My job was to help solve any transaction stumbling blocks before they became problems for Buyers, Sellers, or Agents.

I am a California real estate broker, not an attorney, and this book does not purport to give legal advice, nor is this book a source for tax or insurance advice. For this kind of information, you will need to consult the appropriate professional.

I have been and continue to be an advisor to many real estate attorneys when their clients want clarity on a transaction that has gone wrong. If the real estate dispute results in litigation or arbitration against the real estate Agent, their attorneys may call me. The parties want someone knowledgeable and experienced to testify whether the real estate Agent did their job correctly or not.

In California courts I have been approved as an "expert witness" in real estate matters. This simply means that I can testify and give my opinions about what the real estate licensee either did, or should have done, in a particular situation. The judge, jury, or arbitrators want to determine if the Agent performed properly according to the typical duties of licensees at that time, considering the circumstances and the evidence available. Although this type of work is stressful and complex, I enjoy the challenges. The experience gives me first-hand knowledge of potential lawsuits against Agents.

Probably 90% of these disputes do not actually go to trial, but are mediated or settled between the parties and never become part of case law. I have turned this information into risk management and lawsuit prevention courses for real estate Agents. That's how this book came into being.

California may be the litigation vanguard for the rest of the country. Many real estate practices and regulations start in California, especially as they relate to disclosures of the condition and history of the property. If you are reading this book outside of California, the issues and corresponding recommendations could be parallel, barring local customs and practices. Regardless of the state or country where the property is located, Buyers will want to have all information in order to make an informed decision as to whether to buy or not, and at what price and terms.

This book contains a lot of discussion about disclosure issues. It advises that the more any Buyer knows about what is being purchased, the better it will be for all concerned. Clear, complete, and documented disclosure of all information will typically help protect a Seller against claims after the Buyer takes possession of the property.

HOW THIS BOOK IS ORGANIZED

This book is divided into three sections: Sellers, Buyers, and Escrow Issues. Each section covers a different portion or timeframe in a real estate transaction and addresses red flags which may arise at that stage. Sub-headings organize these sections into specific types of situations or transactions.

If your present transaction seems similar to one of these examples, ☝stop and take a good look at what's going on. Sellers and Buyers will want to talk with their Agents. Agents may want to check with their supervising brokers for suggestions. If major problems are surfacing, engage legal counsel. Protect your clients, yourself, and your company.

You will find that each potential problem issue is followed by suggestions about how you may want to proceed. Although these suggestions are based on current California regulations, they are common-sense enough to apply anywhere. Not all solutions are covered in this book, as the rules change every day. Of course, you may have an additional idea to solve a problem. If you do, let me know and I'll include it in my next book!

Scattered throughout these 100 transactions are extra suggestions, marked as ☞*HINTS*. These can help the above-average Agent to do an even better-than-great job for your clients. These hints may also save you and your clients both money and trouble.

You will also find nine boxed 🗀sidebars which contain summaries of real estate lawsuits or foundation information. I include these as reference sources.

SECTION I addresses situations when working with Sellers to list and market the property. It is the largest section, as Sellers usually have more information than a Buyer, historically and practically, about the property. These examples of red flags suggest how Agents can clarify potential stumbling blocks with Sellers to help the transaction get started on the right course. Both Agents and Sellers will be prepared to inform potential Buyers of any existing issues.

SECTION II covers potentially troublesome situations that may surface when Agents are showing property, writing an offer, and handling the details. Buyers will want to know what questions to ask about the property they are purchasing and what options they have to negotiate.

SECTION III contains examples of issues to consider when Buyers and Sellers have reached agreement and the transaction is "in escrow". Escrow is the process leading up to the transfer of ownership.

In addition to these sections you will also find sidebars containing helpful advisories which you may wish to incorporate into your everyday business practices. I've also included a few summaries of actual lawsuits and what went wrong. Learn what you can from someone else's mistakes!

Let's get started!

SECTION I:
LISTING AND MARKETING PROPERTY

If the Home was Previously on the Market but Didn't Sell

☟ 1.   What reports or inspections were done
          during the prior marketing period?

Each and every report on the property should be made available to
potential Buyers, especially if the reports may have persuaded a prior
Buyer to withdraw from the transaction. If repair estimates or reports
were oral, not written, Sellers may think that doesn't matter. It does! An
unhappy Buyer may uncover that the Seller knew such information and
believe that the Seller hid it. Thorough Agents will advise the Seller to
disclose all flaws and defects of the property, including problems which
were repaired.

Sellers may be worried that a negative report or expensive repair estimate
will scare off a Buyer. Sometimes this is true, and sometimes it is not.
Buyers can and do buy homes with defects, as long as they feel they are
getting what they expect. Buyers don't like it when problems surface
after they have become the new owners, especially if someone knew
about a problem and didn't reveal it. Consider the irate consequences
of a Buyer who discovers the cover-up. "Failure to disclose" is a claim
that frequently creates litigation and expense far beyond the original
cost of repairs.

☞ *Hint: Get all reports in the Seller's possession and make copies for
the file, ready to be given to the next Buyer.*

🖐 2.   Was there a previous offer?

If so, why did the Seller turn it down? Was that offer too low or were there other issues? If the Seller did accept an offer in the past, what caused that transaction to fail? Did the property not appraise at the value expected? Were there issues with repairs or code violations? Did the fault lie with the parties involved? A smart listing Agent will dig into the details to insure a more successful outcome the next time around.

🖐 3.   Does the Seller have any Buyer Exclusions?

Ask questions if you will be the replacement or new listing Agent. Since the home was marketed previously, it may have generated interest from potential Buyers. If a potential Buyer nearly made an offer, or made an offer and then dropped out, the Seller or the former Agent may exclude these particular Buyers from the new listing. Listing agreements may provide a "protection period" to help cover the former Agent's efforts. These named Buyers may work with the former Agent and exclude the present listing Agent from any rights to a commission.

Determining the Seller's Position

🖐 4.   Who is on the Ownership Title?

To prepare for a property to be marketed, it's a good idea to request a Property Profile from your local title company. This "snapshot report" of the property shows who is the owner of record and what loans or liens are secured by the property. Are you working with the real owner? Surprise! Someone deceased is on title, or an ex-spouse. Perhaps the ownership entity is a trust, corporation, or LLC. Make sure your pricing, marketing and listing paperwork is approved and signed by all. This may help avoid disagreement between owners when an offer is presented.

Check the report to see if the status of the property is as represented. If you are representing a sale that includes a separate lot, is the lot a separate parcel on the report? Does the address match what shows up on the report? Does it match the size of the parcel? If there are visually observable easements (see red flag #14), or easements that are supposed to come with the property, they should be there on the record.

Any title issues can be solved, but they take time. Don't wait until an offer is presented. Get on it early, and get the paperwork required to clear the title so escrow can close as agreed.

> ☞ *Hint: Many title companies will produce a Property Profile, or a Preliminary Title Report, without charge if they ultimately issue the policy of title insurance. Check to see what fees may be applicable in your area.*

✋ 5.   Can the Seller Afford to Sell?

Agents may find it helpful to do a "Net Sheet" with the Seller prior to designing a marketing plan. A Net Sheet starts with the possible sales price, deducts the anticipated costs, and projects the estimated proceeds to the Seller. The Seller's costs include the loan and lien payoffs, property taxes, fees, escrow costs, Agent commissions, and other costs of sale. Many Agents do several Net Sheets, using a "best case scenario" with the optimum sales price and a couple of other lesser prices showing the different proceeds. Although these are merely estimates, Sellers can evaluate their position, and Agents can project if there is enough equity to go forward with a sale.

✋ 6.   Did the Seller Take out an Equity Line of Credit?

For many years, these loans had been aggressively marketed to consumers and easy to get. Known as Home Equity Lines of Credit (HELOC), these loans sometimes offered "no costs, no fees, and pay nothing until you take out money against your home's equity". Check the property profile for such a line of credit. Sellers may have overlooked this obligation. They will need to pay off any amounts taken out, plus interest, Lender's fees, and costs to remove this lien. Many owners report being charged such fees even though they never drew money out under the HELOC. These amounts should be subtracted from the Seller's proceeds on the Net Sheet described above.

🖐 7.　Is the Seller is a U.S. Taxpayer?

The Federal Government wants to get its hands on as much tax revenue as possible. Capital gains, which is a tax on a profit made, is normally calculated when Sellers report sales on their tax returns. There is a risk that non-U.S. citizens may sell their property and leave the country, never to file a tax return. Congress passed the Foreign Investment in Real Property Tax Act (FIRPTA) to cut short this practice. Sellers are required to sign a form attesting to their resident status. Unless the Seller is otherwise exempt, the IRS requires that the Buyer hold back an amount to cover the estimated taxes at the time of the sale. In California, the escrow company performs this task and completes the paperwork. FIRPTA regulations require that 10% of the sales price of the property be deducted from the Seller's proceeds and forwarded to the IRS. Naturally, when a tax return is filed, any excess amounts are supposed to be returned by the IRS.

> ☞ *Hint: Certain states, including California, have hold-backs for the state tax burden. There are many exceptions, including owner-occupied homes, so Sellers need to fill out the form to avoid the hold-back. As of this book's publication, California requires 3 1/3% of sales proceeds be withheld from the proceeds and forwarded on to the state tax board. Sellers are entitled to file their tax returns and apply for any refund due them.*

If the Transaction Will be a Short Sale

🖐 8.   Do You Have the Seller's Approval to Contact the Lender?

If the indebtedness and costs to sell exceed the likely selling price (in other words, the Seller owes more than the home is worth) the equity is "short" and this will necessitate a short sale.

Sellers cannot go forward with a sale until they pay off every lien, or debt, against the home. Existing loans against the property are often the largest monetary debt, although IRS tax liens and unpaid judgments are also common. Many of these can be negotiated and reduced if there is enough time and Lender motivation for the sale to happen. Sellers are often embarrassed or too stressed to approach the Lender and ask for a reduction in the debt. It can be time-consuming to determine who currently carries the loan, and where the Lender is located. It may also be difficult to reach a contact person who has any authority to negotiate the loan.

The listing Agent may be able to assist the Seller in these efforts. Before doing so, an Agent should get the Seller's written permission to contact the Lender and initiate communication. Agents should advise the Seller of the Agent's limitations so expectations and time frames can be reasonable.

🖐 9.   Should a Short Sale Listing Addendum be Used?

Sellers need to know that a short sale has increased complexities. Agents should make sure that the Sellers understand the situation. These may include tax consequences, credit consequences, and Lender controls. The Seller also may have to contribute personal funds or agree to pay back a Lender who agrees to reduce the loan so the sale can go through. These items can be spelled out through an addendum to the listing agreement, and will remind the Seller that the Agent cannot give legal or tax advice.

Seller's Title and Escrow Issues

🖐 10.   Is there a Nasty Divorce?

If the selling parties are divorcing, remember to get both signatures on all your paperwork so you don't get blindsided at a later point. A divorce can be stressful, creating antagonism and amnesia. Agents may find themselves working overtime to gain cooperation from the split couple concerning the marketing, disclosures, and sale of their property. The divorcing couple may want their respective attorneys to approve or check the paperwork. They may request additional time to accomplish this task.

Signatures are one important way to verify that each party was in agreement with the paperwork, and with each other. Keep a good log of your communications with the couple. It is important that both Sellers are fully informed and fulfill their obligations per the contract. This will help prevent exposing either one to future liability.

🖐 11.   Can Escrow Divide the Funds?

In California, the escrow is a neutral depository charged with the duty of discharging funds and transferring property title according to the instructions received from the principals. These instructions must agree with one another. Escrow cannot make decisions when caught in the middle of a dispute between parties. If Sellers are divorcing or separating their interests, escrow will disburse funds according to how the paperwork was signed by all owners on title. If they cannot agree, the funds are typically held until the parties agree or a court issues further directions. Agents cannot make such decisions, as they are not a party to the escrow.

> ☞ *Hint: "Of record" means documents which have been filed in the County Recorder's Office where the property is located. Such recorded information is considered to be legal notification to all. If the Seller indicates the existence of an "unrecorded" lien, get the details to avoid future problems.*

🖐 12.   Has One Spouse Remarried?

The husband and wife have divorced, yet are still the owners of record. They are now selling. One of them has remarried. In this situation, the new spouse may have rights under California's community property law, even though that spouse is not on title. Agents will want to advise that the new spouse will be signing a deed relinquishing any interest in the property. It may be a quitclaim deed, which is a type of grant deed. Such a deed will be recorded at the time the Sellers transfer title. It is typically handled through escrow. This paperwork allows the Buyer to purchase with assurance that there should be no claims by a spouse not on record.

☞ *Hint: If there has been a divorce decree and property settlement, yet an ex-spouse still remains on title, the ex-spouse will need to sign a deed to transfer interest to the Buyer.*

🖐 13.   Does the Seller Owe Back Taxes?

A wise listing Agent takes a look at the Property Profile when initially listing the home. If this "snapshot" of the debts against the property shows that the Seller owes state or federal income taxes which are liens against the property, this obstacle may need to be addressed. What is the projected sales price, and will there likely be sufficient funds (net equity) in the property to pay off these debts at the closing? If not, the Seller may need to achieve a reduction either through personal efforts or by hiring appropriate professional help. The IRS maintains a website to answer questions; this may be a first negotiation resource for the Seller. Although real estate Agents do not consider this negotiation as part of their job description, they recognize that these issues will likely create a longer time period to complete the sale. Once an offer is presented, Agents should apprise Buyers of the resultant delays so Buyers may make plans accordingly.

14. What About Easements?

Simply put, easements are rights that others have to use property they do not own. A property may be burdened with an easement, giving others the right to use the owner's property. Easements may or may not be recorded, and in some cases may be created without all parties agreeing to them. Easements exist for many reasons: access, parking, views, trails, open space, utilities, shared driveway, encroachments, etc. Easements vary in description and could be of limited duration or permanent.

Easements are typically complex and are often the subject of disputes. Agents should know that easements may fundamentally affect the right to use property. If an easement shows up on the property profile, ask the title company for an explanation of how it impacts the subject property.

Agents are not expected to be experts in deciphering easements; this requires legal expertise. Agents should not interpret nor represent the implications of existing (or claimed) easements to Buyers.

> *Hint: If you are listing a property that appears to have an encroachment (deck, pool, fence, garage, driveway, etc.) ask questions of the Seller. Is there a mutual agreement with the neighbor? Look at any recorded easements. You may want to advise the Seller to get a lot line survey, since Buyers will want to know what they are buying. Legal counsel, not the Agent, should advise the parties about the next steps to take.*

Disclosures from the Seller

🖐 15. What's the Big Deal with all These Disclosures?

Although it is obvious to real estate Agents, many Sellers cannot fathom why they should tell a Buyer about the problems with their property. Sellers may want to hide the bad stuff from Buyers and from the Agents too. Sellers, after all, want a sale. Perhaps these Sellers do not realize that over 90% of disputes brought by Buyers against Sellers spring from a perceived lack of disclosure. No sale is worth a lawsuit!

The listing Agent has a fiduciary duty of utmost care, integrity, and loyalty to the Seller. This duty requires that Agent to advise the Sellers about their disclosure responsibilities. Consider these Seller questions, and the Agent's correct answer:

- ✓ "Do you think I should say anything about the…" The Agent's answer is YES.

- ✓ "I'm wondering if the Buyer would care about what I did to repair the…" The Agent's answer is YES.

- ✓ "This is not really a big deal, so should I mention the…" Again the Agent's answer is YES.

☞ *Hint: Remind the Seller to repeat this mantra: "If in doubt, disclose!"*

📁 The Case of the Cranky Neighbors

Quick Glimpse of this Case:
The Sellers put their property on the market, partly because their neighbors were openly hostile and abusive towards the Sellers. Physical items as well as verbal insults were tossed back and forth. Police reports were filed. Such animosity might be based on pets, personal prejudices, or past disagreements. Good fences don't always make good neighbors, unfortunately!

Agent Advisory:
First question, is this neighbor animosity a material fact about the property? Secondly, how do you satisfy your duty to disclose it? Third, might you be setting yourself up for trouble if you mention the neighbor's behavior?

Agents are responsible for disclosing anything which could influence the value or desirability of the property. We must disclose all material facts which are not already known to or readily observable by the Buyer. The neighbor's behavior fits this description.

How do you disclose these issues to a potential Buyer? In writing is best, and receipted by the Buyer to prove they got it. Emails work, too. If that's not practical, a verbal disclosure is acceptable as long as you can prove you did so. Notes to your communication log, done at the time you discussed the problem, will help all the parties recall that you did your duty. You may also use a witness to your conversation with the Buyer. Just be ready to prove your disclosure if the Buyer should come back months or years later to say you never told them.

Finally, are you setting yourself up for a personal lawsuit for slander by the neighbor? You are at risk if you state untruths; that's slander. You can state what you personally observed, factually and without malice. If the neighbor caused you a ruckus when you held the house open, you can and should bring this up with potential

Buyers. If you personally didn't experience any disturbance, disclose the problem issues as described by the Seller. State that these observations came from the Seller and have not been personally verified by you (unless they have). The police reports would also back up your obligation to mention the neighborhood disturbance.

Summary:
Disclose what you know, who gave you the information, and whether it has been verified by you or not. If the Buyers don't consider the neighborhood problems important to them, they will buy. If the problems are of concern, the Buyers are probably better off elsewhere. Give the Buyers a contract contingency and sufficient time to meet the neighbors. Let the Buyers determine if they will get along. Fully-informed Buyers typically make a better decision whether to proceed with the purchase or find something else.

Does this issue of problem neighbors reduce the value of the property? Yes, Agents agree it would. The difficult question is by how much? If the neighbor problem is a personal one, likely to end when the Seller moves out, the diminution in value is minimal. If the problem is expected to continue regardless of who moves in, the reduction in value is greater. Buyers are unlikely to choose a home with built-in problems if there are other homes available. Sellers may want to consider giving price or other incentives to attract Buyers.

✋ 16. Does the Seller Balk at the Real Estate Transfer Disclosure Statement?

California law requires that a non-exempt Seller of a property consisting of, or containing, one-to-four residential units provide a signed two page written disclosure checklist to the Buyer. The document is called the Real Estate Transfer Disclosure Statement (RETDS). In it, the present owner notes defects or adverse conditions with the property, whether known or observed.

In addition to the Seller's two pages, the RETDS has a third page for the licensees. Each Agent in the transaction must conduct a diligent visual inspection of the accessible areas, and note their personal observations on this page, or on an attached sheet of paper.

The State of California thinks this form is so important that it gives Buyers a three-day right to rescind (cancel) the transaction. If Buyers receive the RETDS *after* making their offer and find the information is unacceptable, they may back out of the sale. If the RETDS is mailed to the Buyer after making the offer, the time period to rescind is five days from the mailing date. Consider the RETDS as a written "snapshot" a Buyer has of the property's condition, as represented by the Seller and the Agents.

Thus a Seller and the Agents for both Seller and Buyer would be smart to get the RETDS into the Buyer's hands as quickly as possible after the offer is accepted to start the Buyer's cancellation time running.

There are two items to note regarding the above:

A Buyer does not have this same rescission right if the Buyer already has the Seller's disclosure *before* the Buyer made the offer.

In some cases, Sellers are exempt from the requirement to provide a RETDS to Buyers, including a Seller who has obtained the property through the foreclosure process, probate, or other specified court actions or family transfers.

☞ *Hint: Buyers should take a good look at the information contained in the RETDS before spending money on inspections or reports. Inspections can take time and build up costs for the Buyer. Why spend money if you discover something on the RETDS that you simply cannot accept?*

📁 Was There a Material Change with the Property?

In California, the Real Estate Transfer Disclosure Statement (RETDS) must be provided to the Buyer of any one-to-four residential properties. Unless the Seller is otherwise exempt, Sellers must use this two-page check-off sheet with their explanations to tell the Buyers what they know about the property. This form is meant to uncover defects, flaws, and red flags with the property as of the time the Seller fills it out. Things may change over time.

If the Seller or Buyer discovers something not previously disclosed or known, and it is a material fact affecting the value or desirability of the property, it may give the Buyers the right to rescind the transaction. Does the roof now leak after the latest storm? Did the tree in the front yard crash down into the fence? Was there a fire in the property? Has the washer hose sprung a leak? Has an inspection indicated an environmental hazard? Did a report indicate a major component malfunction?

Buyers who receive notice of a newly-discovered material fact have a three-day timeframe for a rescission. If mailed to the Buyers, the timeframe gives five days. Why does this trigger a Buyer's right to rescind the contract? New information constitutes an amended RETDS. If the Buyer didn't know of a new material defect, the Buyer cannot be pressured to buy.

Alternatively, rather than back out, the Buyers may choose to ask the Sellers to make accommodations for the newly discovered defects. The Sellers, however, are not obligated to do so per contract. The options to the Seller may be to either put the property back on the market, or negotiate with the Buyers.

It is unlikely that a Buyer will be forced to buy the property if material defects are discovered after the offer was made. Consider any property in escrow, with all contingencies removed, and a natural disaster strikes. Would the property, now damaged by flood, fire, or earthquake, be forced upon a Buyer? Of course, any disagreements as to what constitutes a "material" fact should be referred to an attorney for a legal interpretation.

✋ 17.   If the Seller Never Lived in the Home, What Good is the RETDS?

If a Seller has never actually lived in the home it will probably impact the helpfulness and usefulness of the RETDS disclosure to a potential Buyer. Non-exempt Sellers are nonetheless required to fill out the form to the best of their knowledge. Non-resident Sellers should check the box "Seller Does Not Occupy the Property" and complete the two-page form, disclosing whatever they do know about the property.

Sellers of rental properties must carefully complete this RETDS disclosure even if they have no hands-on knowledge of the property. They may know of problems through their property manager, renters, or neighbors. Buyers should consider that such non-occupant information provided in the RETDS may be of limited use. Advise the Buyer to get thorough inspections as appropriate.

✋ 18.   What If the Seller Checks "Yes" to Problems, but Doesn't Explain Them?

The Seller's portion of the RETDS disclosure is primarily in a checklist format. There is some limited space to explain answers. Sellers should elaborate on any issues they note. Attach additional pages for explanations as necessary. Much litigation has resulted from Buyers who claim that the Seller was not forthcoming or downplayed the magnitude of a problem. Don't encourage the Seller to hide behind their answers. If Sellers check "yes" to a problem, the details explaining their answers may help protect the Seller from future claims.

🖐 19.   What if the Seller Wants the Agent to Minimize Flaws?

The Real Estate Transfer Disclosure Statement (RETDS) contains a third page that must be filled out by the listing Agent and the selling (Buyer's) Agent. The Agents are charged with the duty to perform a diligent visual inspection of the accessible areas of the property. Don't judge or analyze the flaws you observe as you go through the property, just write them down. If you note everything you observe, large and small, you will be able to demonstrate that you did a diligent inspection.

Agents should not diagnose what may or may not have caused the defects. The front hall light may not work because the bulb is burned out, or it could be because the fixture is broken, or the switch is malfunctioning. You don't have to determine this. Just write down that it doesn't work. Agents do not have a duty to test appliances, crawl under the house, verify condition of the home's components, or otherwise perform an analysis of the property.

This Agent portion of the RETDS is intended to give Buyers the opportunity to have an extra set of eyes scanning the property for obvious problems. In those specific cases where a Seller is *not* required to provide a RETDS, the Agents are still bound to these disclosure duties. This disclosure form for Agents is called the Agents Visual Inspection Disclosure (AVID). Regardless of the Seller's responsibility, Agents are never released from their duty to provide their observations of red flags to the Buyer.

☞ *Hint: It is the Agent's duty to disclose any and all material facts regarding the property which may affect its value or desirability, based on a diligent visual inspection. This duty to disclose does not include the personal or confidential matters of either party, nor to the offered price contemplated by either party.*

✋ 20.   Is the Seller Asking You to Fill Out the Seller's Statement?

If the Seller asks the Agent to fill out the Seller's portion of the Real Estate Transfer Disclosure Statement, this could cause problems. Pages one and two are, after all, the Seller's answers and the Seller's signature verifying the representations. It is extremely unwise for an Agent to complete the Seller's portion, and many real estate firms prohibit their Agents from doing so, with good reason. If an Agent fills out the form with the Seller's direction, Sellers may later claim that the Agent "misinterpreted" or "mistakenly answered" items on the form. Who's the target now?

Sellers may ask the Agent for advice on how to complete the form. Agents should be careful to explain the intent of the form and educate the Seller, but not direct the Seller how to answer. If a Seller is physically or mentally unable to fill out the form, Agents should determine who will be completing the paperwork for the Seller and request that representative take on the task.

✋ 21.   Was there a Death on the Property?

California requires a death on the property within the prior three years to be disclosed (in writing). Note that the death "on" the property is more inclusive than death "in" the property. Swimming pools and yards count.

If the death is a murder or could be considered "notorious", that is, of some wide-ranging public interest, this time frame may be increased. As yourself, will people talk about the tragic event that happened for years to come? If so, disclosure beyond three years may be warranted. Anything that the neighbors will eagerly gossip about to the new Buyer should come from the disclosures provided before the sale was completed.

If the Property is Rural

✋ 22.   Is Something Smelly?

Odors exist, yet are difficult to measure or categorize. Some Buyers crave the sweet smell of the country, while these odors make another's eyes water. Sensitivity levels differ. Wind patterns differ, even within a neighborhood. Sellers are wise to disclose the presence of odors or nearby agriculture or animals that might produce them. If an Agent notes perfume in the air, and the Seller is oblivious, this observation should be provided to the Buyer. Give the Buyers ample opportunity to check it out and determine if the odors are acceptable. The listing Agent has a fiduciary duty of utmost care, integrity, and loyalty to the Seller and such disclosures will be in the Seller's best interest.

✋ 23.   What's the Water Source?

Is the water source a well? Buyers may want to feel confident that a well is producing water at a sufficient rate (gallons per minute) and quality. Get it tested. How old is the well? If the Buyer has plans to expand, does the well produce enough water for such an addition? Are there existing wells on neighboring properties that could impact this property? Is there any chance that prior uses of the property could have caused groundwater contamination or other environmental problems?

24. Is it on a Septic System?

If there is a septic system, does it have the capacity and functionality desired? Where are the leach lines? What's the age and size of the septic tank system? Is it adequate for the present use, and for the number of bedrooms and baths? If the Buyer has plans to expand, will the present septic system be able to handle it? When was the last time the tank was pumped? What are the local codes or requirements to continue to have this septic system in place?

25. Are There Storage Tanks?

Rural property may have aboveground or underground storage tanks for fuel. Are there any stand pipes indicating underground storage tanks? Are these tanks on the property or a neighboring property? Have they been inspected? Fuel tanks may leak, creating environmental hazards that could be costly to remove or repair.

If there are water tanks, have them checked to determine their condition. Is their capacity sufficient for the property? Is the water potable?

☙ 26. Can You Hear Me?

Many Buyers consider data, cable, and cell phone reception important. It may not be available if the property is rural. If this is of concern to your client, it's a good idea to verify what can be provided.

☙ 27. What About Boundaries and Land Use?

Where are the lot lines? Are there any easements? The fence lines may or may not be true indicators of the property's boundaries. Document the zoning and land use. Are there "right to farm" provisions to consider?

Has the land been leased? Is there any chance that the land was used to grow illegal crops or manufacture drugs?

Is the property included in any local "overlay" slated for future use or development? State or federal agencies may also have jurisdiction over the land use. The Buyer may be advised to start these inquiries with the appropriate county or city agency. Agents can accommodate the Buyer and help the Buyer ask the appropriate questions.

> ☞ *Hint: Since rural land may have unclear boundaries and existing fences not built on the lot lines, Agents may want to suggest the Buyer get a lot line survey to determine exactly where the property lines are.*

Area Specific Disclosures

✋ 28.   Are There Local or Regional Disclosures?

Real estate firms may have developed their own disclosures unique to their marketing area or business model. Such disclosures may have been created and disseminated by members of the local real estate association. These disclosures vary as local conditions change. For example, items might include the community's restrictions on water or utility hook-ups, the infestation of certain trees, seasonal road closures, etc. These disclosures inform potential Buyers of unique situations that exist within the area or neighborhood. Agents should ascertain whether or not such area-specific disclosures exist. If there are specific disclosures, use them. Such disclosures will help fully inform Buyers and protect Sellers.

☝ 29.   Is there a Home Owner's Association?

If the home, condo, or townhouse is part of a common interest development (CID), there will likely be a Homeowner's Association (HOA) responsible for providing services and overseeing the common facilities. This HOA may govern the appearance and use of the properties within the community, often through the issuance of Covenants, Conditions and Restrictions (CC&R's). These CC&R's may control an unlimited number of issues, such as the location and number of parking spaces, storage lockers, window coverings, mailboxes, satellite dishes, exterior paint colors, and so forth. Additionally, an HOA may be the entity that contracts for and manages overall services delivered to the properties within the community, such as landscaping, exterior maintenance, utilities, fire & liability insurance, and the like. Every HOA differs. Ask the Seller for the contact who can provide information about what items are included in the monthly fee.

> ☞ *Hint: The CC&R's described above usually control anything modifying or adding to the exterior of the properties in the common interest development. Buyers should read them carefully to avoid surprises.*

☝ 30.   Can the Seller Provide HOA Documents?

In addition to the Covenants, Conditions and Restrictions (CC&R's), which are typically recorded and available through the title company, a listing Agent will want to advise the Seller to obtain other documents pertinent to the HOA. These documents are not likely matters of record. They may include copies of the current Rules and Regulations, minutes of prior HOA meetings, and reserve projections. A reserve fund should be built up over time to cover the cost of major improvements eventually needed. Sometimes the HOA does not budget for these. Budget shortfalls, and the resultant assessments, have caused many new owners to feel shortchanged. The Seller will want to ready these documents so the Buyer can review and approve them in ample time. If there are to be transfer fees to the potential Buyer, the HOA should be able to give this information to the Seller.

When the Seller Did Construction Work on the House

👋 31.   What Was Done?

Agents should ask a lot of questions if the Seller has renovated, repaired, expanded, or otherwise remodeled the property. Here is a starter list:

> ☞*Hint: It is very unwise for the Agent to represent or advertise a property as "totally" remodeled. The word may connote too many issues to be accurate.*

- ✓ What is the Seller's description of work that was done? How long ago was it done?

- ✓ Was it to repair a problem or something else? Has the problem been solved?

- ✓ Was there an insurance claim made with regard to the work done?

- ✓ Was all the work done with permits?

- ✓ Who did the work, and were they appropriately licensed? Can the Seller provide a list of names and contact information of those who did the work?

- ✓ Was all construction done to current code, and if so, who verified that it meets current code?

- ✓ Was any work started but not completed? Is there any problem that showed up but was *not* addressed?

- ✓ Have the "sign offs" or notices of completion with the building department been done?

- ✓ Has all of the work been paid for?

✓ Are there any mechanic's liens filed against the property?

✓ What paperwork, reports or estimates does the Seller have in their possession?

This information should be noted in the listing Agent's file and delivered to the Buyer.

☞ *Hint: The Agent may want to recommend that the Buyer go to the local building permitting authority to make sure there are no further issues with the property.*

✋ 32.   Were there Water Intrusion Issues?

This is a real hot button, as water where it's not supposed to be may lead to mold. Inquire whether the Seller has had any flooding, water intrusion, leaks, burst pipes or washer hoses, etc. Ask whether the Seller made any insurance claims regarding water issues. If such claims were recent, the Buyer might have problems getting homeowner's insurance from certain insurance companies. A lack of insurance may cause the Buyer's Lender to withhold funding. When you list the property, find out whether or not any leaks have been repaired.

Flooding is another potential problem issue. If the property appears to be below the grade level of the surrounding streets or properties, ask questions and have the Seller make full disclosure of any items. It may also be appropriate for the Agent to note their observations on their section of the RETDS or AVID forms.

> ☞*Hint: A Seller who paints over the signs of a leak that has been repaired should make certain to disclose the repair to the Buyer. The Buyer should get full inspection of water intrusion questions. Leaks have a tendency to re-appear!*

✋ 33.   Did the Seller Recently Buy this Property?

If the Seller purchased within the last year or two, the listing Agent should ask for copies of any and all reports, inspections, and estimates made during the time of ownership. Although it may seem that an old report is of no value, particularly when there is a newer report done, the Buyer should be the one to decide. It is possible that old reports reveal work that was not yet done, or problems not yet repaired or addressed. The Buyer may want to use the old reports as an assurance that no issues remain. The Seller's delivery of all reports, old or new, can help protect against claims that the Buyer was not fully informed.

> ☞*Hint: Ask the Seller what reports and other information the Seller was given by the prior owners. Advise the Seller to disclose these material facts to subsequent Buyers.*

🖐 34.   Should the Agent Order Inspection Reports for the Seller?

A good listing Agent may advise the Seller to head off surprises by ordering inspection reports at the time the listing is being prepared. This practice can be helpful to give the Seller time to correct repairs. Sellers can direct any necessary work and reduce the potential of the Buyer negotiating the purchase price.

Agents should be cautious about advising Sellers which inspection or repair companies to use. This is important whether the Seller orders reports pre-sale or after an offer has been accepted. An Agent's recommendations of a service provider may carry an implied, and unintended, responsibility. If the service provider misses something or does an inadequate job, the Agent may be blamed for causing the problem. Agents should give their clients the names of at least three service providers and let the client select whom to use. Document the client's selection and obtain the authority to order the requested report.

> ☞*Hint: If your client will be absent at the time of inspection, you may be asked to deliver the Seller's or Buyer's check when the inspector appears at the home. Even though the check may be made out to a third party, current California Trust Fund regulations state that these checks are trust funds. If the aggregate amount of checks you handled for your client reaches $1000, you must keep a written log of all checks and their disposition.*

Marketing the Property

📂 When the Market is Changing Fast, What Price is Right?

Sellers are in control of the prices they ask for their homes. If the market is moving up fast and homes are turning over quickly, Sellers may expect an unreasonable jump in values and Buyers may pay it. If the market has slowed and not all homes are selling, Sellers may set prices in line with their competition yet their properties remain unsold. How do successful Agents help Sellers position their asking prices so sales can result?

Pricing is the most important part of a successful sale. Price may overcome difficulties in condition, location, availability, or rising interest rates. The correct price can make a sale happen quickly. The wrong price may cause a lot of wasted time and effort for both Agent and Seller.

The selling price of a home is not determined by what Sellers, Agents, Lenders, insurers, or appraisers think. It's set by what a Buyer is willing to offer. As is often said in our industry, "The right price is the one that walks in the front door". Buyers figure out what to offer by asking their real estate Agent for comparable information on other homes. Buyers always want to know the home's asking price, how long it's been on the market, and the extras. Since Agents and Buyers know this data, shouldn't the Sellers know everything, too?

Use a Competitive Market Analysis (CMA) to show what competing homes are currently for sale, what homes have recently sold and how long these homes took to sell. Also indicate homes which did not sell, as these were "fantasy" prices which didn't interest any Buyers.

Have a discussion with the Sellers about who sets the price. The Seller chooses the price they want to ask, with the information you provide.

The Seller is also in charge of the showing condition of the property. The Agent controls the marketing, promotion, and negotiation. The final determination of the price negotiated and paid, however, is controlled by the Buyers.

Why is accurate pricing of a home so critical?

Even slightly overpricing the home reduces the number of showings significantly, by as much as half, because Buyers won't want to see homes too far above their target price range. In addition, no Buyer's Agent wants to show overpriced homes when there are better values available elsewhere.

Pricing it at market encourages Agents to show a listing to Buyers when their "wish list" matches the Seller's asking price range.

Pricing it under the market gives highest exposure, as Agents know it is worth showing a well-priced home, even if it isn't the perfect home, to Buyers. If the home is considered an excellent value, it's shown frequently until someone snaps it up.

Agents don't decide which homes sell.

Agents do prioritize and decide which homes to *show* their Buyers. Agents will always put the better-valued homes at the top of the list, thereby giving these homes the greatest exposure. For a home to be sold, it has to be shown!

Remind Sellers that they are in a good position if Buyers make offers on their home, regardless of the offer presented. Receiving an offer does not commit Sellers to sell at the offered price. They can always turn down an offer if it is not right for them. *Sellers, however, cannot turn down an offer if they don't have one!* Isn't it better to have offers to consider, and possibly counter-offer, than to have no offers at all?

What are the disadvantages to the Agent of overpricing a listing?

Disgruntled Sellers blame you for their home not selling.
Buyers think you are poorly informed about values.
Agents bear the continuing costs to advertise and promote the listing.
Open houses will be awkward, since the listing Agent represents the Seller and cannot suggest a lower price to Buyers who walk in.
Other Sellers will wonder why it takes your listings so long to sell.
Agents will think you aren't knowledgeable about your area.
You will be stressed when Sellers ask, "Why haven't you sold my house yet?"
Since your listing is overpriced, it will be used to make the competition look good.
Buyers will make lowball offers when a home has been hanging around the market for a long time.

Compare Agent previews (cards left at the home) to actual showings (appointments to show the home to Buyers). If Agents aren't coming back to show the home after previewing, you can bet it's an issue of the price being too high. Agents have "disqualified" your listing.

Even if a Buyer were to make a "high" offer, there are two things which must happen for the transaction to be able to successfully close escrow:

> The Buyer must qualify for the loan, and

> The home must appraise at what the Buyer is willing to pay.

Overpriced homes may be shown by Agents to make the competing homes look well-priced by comparison. An overpriced home may help Buyers make up their minds to purchase another home. What stress! Sellers struggle to keep their home in "showable" condition, arranging their schedules to accommodate potential Buyers, and it drags on and on.

The advantages to the Seller in marketing the home at the right price include:

Faster sale
More Buyers competing
Seller typically nets a higher price as a result
Offers come in with fewer contingencies
Less pressure to negotiate during inspections
Seller can control terms more easily
Less hassle for Seller to keep home "showable" while living there
Shorter time on the market
The Seller's home is not used to sell the other properties on the market.
Avoids becoming "shopworn" and attracting "lowball Buyers"

Let the Seller know! Prepare your Competitive Market Analysis research to give you a foundation of strength and market knowledge you want the Seller to understand. The CMA data is all verifiable and can be prepared easily in advance. Let Sellers know all the data, discuss the above-mentioned points, and guide them to the correct decision.

✋ 35.   Is your License Number on Your Marketing Material?

Current California law requires that real estate licensees put their license number on all promotional materials intended to be disseminated to the public. This includes business cards. Property signs and generic websites (those not touting a particular property) are presently excluded from this law. Once the marketing has been successful, and an offer comes in, both of the Agents' license numbers must be on the sales contract documents.

✋ 36.   Can the Flyer Cause Problems?

Flyers, brochures, multiple listing data, internet postings, and the like are intended to promote the property and attract potential Buyers. This information is expected to be reliable and accurate; presenting the best of the property without the details of its flaws. Although these promotional pieces are not intended to be part of the actual negotiated transaction, Agents have been caught up in litigation because of what was represented. Blatant errors have caused Buyers to seek compensation. Once the advertisement or promotional piece is complete, present it to the Seller for verification and approval. Do the same for data put into the multiple listings or internet. If the Agent has made an error, the Seller may be a source to correct it prior to disseminating the information.

37. Won't the Disclaimers Protect Against Claims?

Agents may mistakenly feel reassured by the preprinted "standard" disclaimer at the bottom or end of promotional pieces. The disclaimer may state that the information may not be accurate, and that the reader should verify the facts and not rely on the Agent's representations contained in the piece. It may be that the disclaimer is buried in or tagged onto the information. This is no shield to protect the Agent who pumps out inaccuracies.

In cases where the information is questionable, and the Agent's intent is to caution the reader that the information may not be as represented, a disclaimer is appropriate. Such a disclaimer should be specific to what aspect of the property is being disclosed, and printed in a similar size type as the questionable condition. A specific disclaimer will help Sellers and listing Agents do their best to alert a Buyer about what is known and what is not.

> ☞*Hint: When making a representation about the property, state the source of your information and whether or not you verified it. Here's an example: "According to (whom - the Seller, the assessor, the neighbor, the planning department, etc.) the situation is (give the disclosure). Agent has confirmed/verified this with (whom or what entity)." Alternatively you might state: "Agent has not verified this."*

38. What About Seller Confidences?

Sellers are motivated to sell or they wouldn't go to the trouble of putting their property on the market. Why are they selling? The listing Agent may have an intimate knowledge of the Seller's situation. Whether the Seller's motivation is financial pressures, divorce, lifestyle changes, health, profit taking, or anything else, this personal information should remain confidential unless it could impact the value or desirability of property itself.

Agents need to remain clear about what details are material to the value or desirability of the property and what details are not. If the Seller allows or encourages the Agent to reveal motivation to potential Buyers, be sure to document the Seller's permission.

🖐 39.   Open Houses – Can You Hire a Surrogate?

Due to time or schedule conflicts, an Agent may be unable to hold a listed home open to potential Buyers. If the Agent engages someone to be present at the Open House, there are several options. If a substitute, licensed Agent from the same firm holds the home open, this Agent may perform the duties of the listing Agent. The Agent is the fiduciary of the Seller. In this case, dual agency will ensue if the Buyer purchases the home through the open house Agent.

If the Agent present works for another firm, there is no fiduciary duty to the Seller. Such an Agent may represent potential Buyers in single agency. Buyers should be informed of the agency relationships which are available, and choose accordingly.

☞ *Hint: In California, unlicensed representatives may only hand out a flyer or brochure and may not engage in any activities which would constitute "selling" the property. This includes showing property or discussing the terms or conditions of a potential sale.*

🖐 40.   Is the Seller a Real Estate Licensee?

Sellers may have a real estate license, either active or inactive. If so, this status should be indicated to the Buyer. Licensees are perceived to have superior knowledge compared to the general public in matters involving real estate. You wouldn't want the Buyer claiming that the Seller took unfair advantage, right? Protect the Seller by advising that any licensed status be disclosed to the Buyer. This is typically written in as part of the real estate transaction paperwork.

✋ 41.   Does the Seller Want You to Illegally Discriminate?

If you find yourself listing a property with a Seller who states an intention to sell to "the right kind of people", get yourself on high alert. Sellers who select a Buyer based on the Buyer's race, color, religion, sex, ancestry, physical handicap, national origin, or marital status are treading on extremely dangerous ground. Such discriminatory practice is against both state and federal fair housing laws, as well as common sense.

Agents who assist a Seller in eliminating (or accepting) offers based on discriminatory criteria may find themselves embroiled in costly and time-consuming litigation. Do the right thing. Advise Sellers to consider all offers based on each proposal's financial and business merits. The Seller may select an offer based on many different aspects, including the Buyer's creditworthiness and financial strength, when title will transfer, personal property issues, and the like. These are reasonable considerations. If a Seller asks you to solicit information about the Buyer's race, color, religion, national origin, sex, ancestry, handicap, or marital status, inform the Seller that such a request may expose the Seller to violations of the California Business and Profession Code, Department of Real Estate regulations, and HUD regulations. Protect your Seller, and protect yourself.

Is your Listing Tenant Occupied?

🖐 42.   What Rights does the Tenant Have?

This is an involved topic. Agents should take extra care when listing and marketing a rental property. Ask the Seller for a copy of the rental agreement or lease, and inquire whether there have been any modifications of these items or any oral agreements. Follow these recommendations to clarify how to proceed:

The Buyer may intend to occupy the property and evict the present tenant. If so, find out about local rent control laws and what rights the tenant may have to continue occupancy or receive a notice to vacate. Do not assume that new owners can do what they want with the property. If there is a lease or rental agreement in effect, it is likely that such an agreement needs to be honored even past the date title transfers. If the community where the property is located has rent control laws, there may be restrictions on the rent that can be charged by a new owner. An Agent is in the best position to learn about how such regulations will affect the sale of the property. Due to the complexities of local rent control regulations, it will be necessary to consult a legal advisor to determine the rights of the parties in possession.

☞ *Hint: If a tenant-occupied property is foreclosed, the existing lease or rental agreement may be invalidated. The foreclosing owner may give the tenant notice to vacate but must follow state-mandated timeframes.*

✋ 43.   Why Should the Tenant Cooperate?

Consider that tenants see no benefit, and many difficulties, when their residence is put on the market. Tenants understand that a sale may mean that they will have to move out. The renter may be less than thrilled with a parade of people coming through to view the home, interrupting schedules and violating privacy. A wise Agent contacts the tenant at the outset to open a dialog about what to expect. Earn the respect and cooperation of the tenant.

When the property is put on the market, what's in it for the tenant to cooperate? Some Agents have offered a reduced rent while the property is for sale to compensate the renter for their inconvenience. Unfortunately, this may backfire and encourage the renter to prolong the marketing period, since the rent subsidy will continue.

A better plan might be to offer the renter an incentive once an offer is accepted, or when the title transfers. This bonus could be conditioned upon the cooperation of the renter during showings, open houses, etc.

✋ 44.   Do You Want to Use a Key Box in a Tenant-Occupied Property?

Will the renter allow the convenience of a key box on the property? If so, there may be theft issues which are difficult to dispute. A Seller's homeowner's insurance policy typically does not cover a tenant's claims. It may be advisable to secure renter's insurance to cover the possibility of damage or loss during the marketing period.

45. Will the Tenant Verify the Lease Situation?

Once there is an acceptable offer, it is advisable to get written estoppels from the tenants. Estoppels are tenant-signed forms that verify the terms of the lease. These forms cover the renter's status, and include confirmation of current rent, security deposits, other deposits, length of lease, and such. Based on these estoppels, the escrow company will be able to apportion rents, as well as credit the rental deposits to the Buyer from the Seller's proceeds.

Estoppels will also help assure the prospective Buyer that the tenant has no current offsets to rents or claims against the Seller. Without estoppels, undisclosed claims could end up being the Buyer's problems. Not good! A copy of the lease or rental agreement is usually attached to the signed estoppels from the tenant. Estoppels help avoid future misunderstandings between the present tenants and the new Buyer.

Prepare the Seller for Offers

🖐 46.   Is a Bidding Scenario Possible?

The practice of the real estate industry is to present offers to the Seller as soon as they are received. An Agent sometimes alters that plan. An Agent may wish to market a desirable property by advertising that offers will not be presented until a future fixed date. The intent of this strategy is to give time to expose the property to more potential Buyers and thus produce more competing offers. Multiple offers in a hot market are expected. Multiple offers in a stable or soft market may arise when the property is well-priced at or below comparable properties.

If an Agent plans to hold off on the presentation of offers, discuss the strategy to get the Seller's approval. Any marketing plan may have downsides. Be sure the Seller understands the risks. What risks? A Buyer may want to make an offer but is unable to wait until the date specified to open the offers. Buyers and their Agents may opt out of the bidding wars. When the time comes to present offers, there may be none to present! Let the Seller endorse the marketing plan you envision.

☞ *Hint: If you choose to prepare multiple counter offers, use care when completing the forms. Do not inadvertently cause the Seller be in contract with two Buyers. Check with your company's policy to determine how to proceed and which forms are in use.*

47. Can You Buy Your Own Listing?

You can, but do so with full disclosure and a lot of caution. Whom do you represent? You are the fiduciary of the Seller. You would also be the fiduciary of the Buyer, yourself. The problems are obvious. If anything is out of order, it's likely your fault. If the Seller has any complaints, your neck may be in the noose. If you have the listing, representing the Seller is priority #1. A better way to buy the property is to decline the representation of the Seller. Let another Agent do it. No commission is worth a lawsuit.

SECTION II:
WORKING WITH BUYERS

📁 Qualify Buyer Prospects so you Don't Spin Your Wheels

It's exciting to come across a prospect who wants to buy a home with you. Before you start working for them you'll want to determine if a Buyer is ready to go, and is a good match for the help you can give. If not, you may be wasting your time and resources. Ask yourself, are theses Buyers <u>prospects</u>, or are they <u>suspects</u>?

When I was new in the real estate business, there were many Buyers who frustrated me. I previewed homes, mapped out showing appointments, and spent days and weeks showing them homes that fit their requests. I gave up many social opportunities because these prospects wanted to see homes after hours and weekends, whenever their work schedule allowed. I went months without any of them actually making an offer. Some were simply not ready to purchase; some only wanted decorating ideas; some thought it was interesting to see other people's homes. There were Buyers who looked at the homes I selected, found what they wanted, and wrote up their offer with their brother-in-law or buddy. I remember working an entire weekend showing homes to one couple. We had narrowed it down to two possibilities. They told me they would let me know what they wanted to do the next day. When I called them to ask what they had decided, they announced "We have reached a decision, Cari. We are going to buy a new BMW instead of a house. We really thank you for your help in letting us see what was on the market." A-a-a-a-arrrrgh!

My lack of success made me depressed and nearly drove me out of real estate as a career. What was I missing? Eventually, I realized that I was not asking enough of the right questions *before* I went to work for these prospects. Just as they were able to select me, I was able to select them. Were these prospects a good match for my skills, time, and efforts? I began asking what they expected, and when. I screened them and worked for only those prospects truly needing my assistance. Instead of dead-end failure, I began having success. Experience taught me that there were four different categories of questions to ask. Here's where I started:

1. Are They Able to Complete a Transaction?
Who's the decision maker? Do they have the final say? Is there a "terminator" lurking in the background ready to sabotage the transaction?

Who will be making the offer? Who will be signing your paperwork? Have these Buyers been pre-approved? Where's their down payment and is it ready to go?

2. How Flexible Are They?
There is rarely a home that meets 95% of a Buyer's needs and wants. A 90% solution is fantastic, and an 80% to 85% match is the most likely home that any Buyer can hope to find. Do your Buyers understand that they will probably have to give up on some aspect of what they want? Work with realistic Buyers.

Are they location specific? Are they property type specific? Perhaps they are really focused on the size of the home? Is price the deciding point? Help them prioritize. You can find a home that meets certain of their needs, but they may have to give up on other criteria. The more open-minded they are, the better their chances to get a match.

Speaking of price, are Buyers being realistic? Is what they want available at their budget? If financing is tight, do they have any other sources of down payment?

3. What's Their Motivation?
What are the Buyers' time deadlines? How long have they been looking? How soon do they need to find a home? Can they stay where they are indefinitely? If so, they may not be very motivated.

Have they seen other homes they liked? If so, what did they do? If they made an offer, what was the outcome?

Can they move quickly when the right home comes on the market? Are they available to you when you need them?

Use "What if?" questions, such as "What if the home you want isn't available at your price? What will you do?" Their answers will help you determine if they are really ready to buy, or merely thinking about it.

Another excellent motivation question is "If a home that suited your needs came on the market tomorrow, is there anything that would prevent you from making an offer?" The Buyers' answers will show you their true time motivation. Some Buyers will answer "I'd make an offer" and others will tell you "Well, that's not going to work for us until later". Know what you're facing.

4. Are They Willing to Give You Some Control?
Will they sign the Agency Disclosure Form with you? Although this is not a contract, it indicates a willingness to work with you. If they hesitate to sign receipt of a one-page disclosure, what makes you think that they trust you enough to sign a multi-page binding sales agreement with you? It's possible they don't intend to work with you at all.

Many Buyers choose to hire their Agents through use of a Buyer Broker Agreement. It is a binding contract. Some agreements provide for compensation from the Buyers and some do not. Any Seller-offered compensation will usually offset the fee owed by the Buyers, if your contract provides for it.

A Buyer Broker Agreement creates a fiduciary agreement between the Buyers and your firm. It can give you incentive to search out all homes that suit your Buyers. It allows you to approach an owner who is selling without benefit of a real estate Agent and be assured of a commission, since the Buyer has agreed to pay you.

Where do you start?

Buyers are in the market for a limited time. Buyers may think it's a good idea to have several different Agents in the same area looking for them. As you know, this can backfire for them. A Buyer working with several Agents is less likely to be called first when a terrific home comes on the market, since each of these Agents may have a favorite Buyer to call.

Ask if your Buyer prospect would agree to work with you exclusively for just two weeks. You will prioritize them and their needs. If you can't find anything that suits them, you will each be free to go elsewhere. During those two weeks, however, they will call you with any ad they see that they like, they will contact you if they see a sign on a home, and they will be provided with access to daily updates about what's on the market. Naturally, when the two weeks are up, you can choose to continue to help them if they are mutually inclined.

These are just starting suggestions, of course. There are many other questions to develop your skills in explaining what you do, and what you don't do. Spend more time pre-counseling and bonding with potential Buyers. What do they need? What do they want? What will they do to reach their goals? Understanding who they are, and what they need is the most professional way to accomplish a satisfying transaction.

ꗧ 48. What if the Prospect Balks at an Agency Disclosure?

The Agency Disclosure is a disclosure, not a contract. The wording on this document clearly states that the prospect is acknowledging *receipt* of the form, nothing more. The Agency Disclosure form does not bind you to the prospect, nor them to you.

Agents may choose to use the Agency Disclosure as a filter to determine if the potential client really wants their services or not. Many Agents present this form to their prospects before they get started providing real estate services. It offers Agents the opportunity to explain how they work, and what duties are owed to Buyers and Sellers. The Agent can discuss the representation a prospect might ultimately want, whether single or dual agency.

The prospect may sign the disclosure, or decline to do so. If the prospect declines, you may choose to work with prospects more eager for your help. A prospect who refuses to sign that they received the Agency Disclosure from you may not truly plan to work with you. Ask questions to determine why there is reluctance.

The Agency Disclosure must be presented, and signed, prior to the Agent obtaining any other signatures on listings, offers, or other paperwork. Keep a copy of the signed form in your transaction file.

> ☞*Hint: Ask the prospective Buyer if they are working with another real estate Agent. If you find out what happened with that relationship it may help you decide what to do next. Avoid issues of procuring cause where the Agents dispute who produced the transaction.*

♈ 49. Has the Prospect Signed other Agency Disclosure Forms?

Buyers and Sellers may sign the Agency Disclosure with more than one Agent, according to how many Agents are assisting them in their transactions. The form does not have a beginning or termination date, just a date for when it was receipted. Prospective Buyers may acknowledge signing other forms with other Agents, according to the areas where they are looking for property. Although the Agency Disclosure is neither a contract nor a commitment, it may help clarify whether the prospect plans to work with you or has someone else waiting in the wings. Ask questions!

♈ 50. Does a Buyer-Broker Agreement Exist?

A Buyer may wish to engage your services with a written Buyer representation agreement. Such an agreement provides a fee if you perform your specified duties and are successful in locating a suitable property. This agreement may or may not include an upfront retainer for your services. Agents who sign such a contract with the Buyer should make certain to perform their obligations as agreed.

Buyer representation agreements are also useful when the property being purchased is a short sale, and the Lender controls the fee paid to the listing Agent and consequently shared with the Buyer's Agent. Lenders have no control over what a Buyer may choose to pay their own Agent under a separate representation agreement.

🖐 51.   Does the Buyer Believe the Agent is "Theirs"?

If the listing with a real estate firm is sold by another licensee within the firm or its branch offices, dual agency is created (see following Sidebar). The real estate firm, or agency, will be the fiduciary of both the Seller and the Buyer. Seller and Buyer may have two different licensees (people) representing them within the firm, but it is still considered dual agency. This is allowable under California law, as long as disclosure of the situation is made and agreed to by the parties. Once the Buyer decides to buy a listing already marketed through the same firm, the Agent should verify that the Buyer is informed and agreeable that the firm represents the Seller's interests as well. To ignore this step may create a situation that attorneys refer to as "undisclosed dual agency". It's costly!

🗁 Understanding the Agency Disclosure Form

If a property is or contains one-to-four residential units, California law provides that Agents provide the principals with an Agency Disclosure form. This one page (two-sided) form spells out the different duties and obligations owed by a Seller's Agent, Buyer's Agent, or Dual Agent. It explains the differences between single agency and dual agency. Buyers and Sellers date and sign that they have received this form. The back of the form contains the pertinent section of the Civil Code printed in light ink, and does not have to be signed.

Agents give this form to clients prior to obtaining any signatures on other real estate documents. The Seller signs one for the listing Agent prior to the listing agreement, and also receives a second form from any Agents bringing in an offer. Buyers sign this Agency form before they sign any offer to purchase or other documents. Buyers and Sellers may receive this form from more than one Agent, depending upon the number of Agents assisting them in their transaction.

Dual Agency

If you are an Agent bringing in an offer for a Buyer, and the property is listed with another Agent in your company, this transaction will make you a dual Agent. How does that change what each Agent can and cannot do?

Being a dual Agent requires you to perform fiduciary duties to both parties...the Buyer and the Seller. When your company represents both the Buyer and the Seller, the Agents (referred to in the form as *associate licensees*) are automatically dual Agents, even though the listing Agent may never meet the Buyer, or the Buyer's Agent may never meet the Seller.

The "Agent" under the law is the company broker as registered with the Department of Real Estate. Some companies have both corporate-owned offices and franchised offices. In this case, the individual franchise offices are separate from the corporate offices and not considered the same "Agent" representation. Branch offices of the same ownership are considered one "Agent" and all the associate licensees in these offices are considered as one entity.

If you bring in an offer on one of your company's listings, you become a dual agent, and must represent your Buyer, *and the other associate licensee's Seller*, in a fiduciary manner, with utmost care, integrity, honesty and loyalty. The associate licensee who has the listing must represent your Buyers with the same duty of utmost care, integrity, honesty and loyalty. That's saying a lot.

Lawsuits Focus on the Duties Owed to the Fiduciaries

Most lawsuits center on the subject of agency. Whenever there's an unhappy Buyer or Seller, the attorneys investigate if the Agents did their jobs. The basics of an Agent's responsibilities are primarily contained in the Agency Disclosure form. This California law is written into Civil Code Section 2079.

Writing an Offer on a Company Listing

If you are writing the offer for your Buyers on a company listing, you will be a dual Agent. You can't work against the best interests of the Seller. You have to give the Seller all the details which will help the Seller make their best deal, with the exception of any price discussions or confidential non-material information you may know about the Buyers.

If you are a dual Agent, negotiating one side *against* the other will violate the fiduciary duties owed to your clients, since you represent both. Strategies are limited when you represent both sides. A dual Agent has a fiduciary duty of utmost care, integrity, honestly and loyalty to both Buyer and Seller.

It is definitely a delicate balance to represent both Buyer and Seller when each has a different goal in their transaction. A dual Agent cannot be an advocate for one party. It's possible to accomplish this, but it is very tricky. Many states do not allow it.

Confidences May Not be Material Facts
Personal details about the Buyer's situation, or the Seller's, may be kept confidential if these details do not materially affect the value or desirability of the property. This might be difficult to determine. For example, if the Buyer tells you something in confidence about his personal situation, *and it will impact the Buyer's ability to close escrow on time,* you need to inform the Seller. The timing of the close of escrow is a material fact. However, if the Seller confides his desperate situation about selling, his motivation or debts, you can't relay this insider information to your Buyer. That would be disloyal to the Seller.

Do Dual Agents have to tell Both Parties Everything?
The Agency Disclosure states that the *only* information that dual Agents are not obligated to share with the other parties is that which is confidential or concerns price. A dual Agent can't relay to a Buyer that a Seller will sell for less, even if the Seller (or the Seller's Agent) told the Agent so. It is disloyal and a breach of agency duties for a listing Agent to quote a price less than the listing price. Of course, Sellers may take less than the asking price. A good plan for listing Agents is to simply say "Seller will carefully consider all offers. Write it up and I'll be happy to work with you to present your Buyer's offer." As an alternative, if the Seller is willing to take less, get a written price reduction.

One final note: Any and all *material facts* which affect the value or desirability of the property must be disclosed to the Buyer, whether dual agency exists or not. That includes anything which concerns the sticks and stones of the home, or the land, or the neighborhood, or anything else addressed in the contract or on the Transfer Disclosure Statement. "If in doubt, disclose" is a good mantra to remember.

✋ 52.   Don't You Need Paperwork to Create Agency?

Agency and its fiduciary responsibilities can be created by writing, words, or deeds. It can be created unintentionally even if no paperwork is presented or signed. Whether an agency relationship was created may be a matter of legal opinion.

If you don't intend to be the Agent of the Buyer or Seller, don't give verbal reassurances to the contrary. Examples of statements that may indicate the licensee intends to represent a principal might include the following:

> "Don't worry. I will take care of this for you."
> "I'm happy to assist you with this transaction."
> "I can handle this sale and give you all the help you need."

If the Seller does not have his or her own real estate or legal advisor, use care when representing a Buyer's offer to this Seller. You may inadvertently create a dual agency situation. This is possible, for example, when a property is for sale by owner. Make certain that the Seller understands that you are the Agent and fiduciary of the Buyer, and not the Seller. Advise the Seller to get a real estate advisor.

✋ 53.   If They Don't Pay Me a Commission,
         How Can I be Their Agent?

Payment of a fee or commission does not of itself create an agency relationship. A Buyer's Agent may receive a commission paid by the Seller and shared through the listing Agent, yet not be the Seller's Agent. Conversely, agency duties can be created even if there is no fee paid! You want to handle the sale of your Mom's house, and not charge her for your help? Good for you! Of course, in representing her you may find yourself in the capacity referred to as "gratuitous agency". All the fiduciary duties owed, with none of the income. In short, agency may be unintended and created by what you say or do.

Showing Properties

✋ 54. Is the Agent Unfamiliar with this Area?

Agents licensed by the state are permitted to handle real estate transactions anywhere within the state, but an Agent who considers this to be legal protection and approval is walking into a trap. The licensee has the fiduciary duty to represent a client with utmost care and integrity coupled with the diligent exercise of reasonable skill and care. Can a licensee know the unique aspects of this region? The answer is, probably not!

If your clients ask for your help with a transaction not in your area, you have several options:

❖ Do the transaction (and bankroll your attorney if something goes wrong). This approach is not recommended.

❖ Decline to do the transaction yourself, and refer the transaction to a licensee who has expertise in that area. Referral fees may be appropriate.

❖ Bring in the services of a licensee who has the desired expertise, and work together as a team. This offers the chance to share the fees and expand your base of knowledge.

In any case, let your clients know that you appreciate the trust they are putting in you. Advise them of your limitations, and what you intend to do to make sure they get the best service.

✋ 55.   Is the Agent Unfamiliar with this Type of Property?

Your clients may have entrusted you to help with their home. Now they want to have your personality and thoroughness to assist them in buying an investment property, securing a commercial lease, or handling another non-residential transaction. If you have no background or expertise with the potential transaction, follow the same options listed above. Expand your knowledge without jeopardizing your license.

📁 This Transaction Exceeded Abilities from the Start

Case Summary:
The Buyers successfully owned and managed a duplex for several years, and were ready to build their empire. They asked their friend and Agent to find them something bigger to trade into. Their Agent had never sold anything larger than a duplex, nor had the Agent's broker.

A 20-unit apartment came on the market in a depressed neighborhood. The Buyers' Agent showed the exterior of the apartment building and touted the incredibly low price per unit. The price was right, the rental market was hot, and the Buyers made an offer. The listing Agent and Seller prepared an incredibly detailed and thorough 250-page disclosure package and provided these to the Buyers' Agent. It seems the building had many ongoing problems with tenants' lawsuits against the property owner, evictions, maintenance issues, etc.

The Buyers' Agent gave the disclosure package to the Buyers, who "signed off" without reading them. The Buyer's Agent did not offer to explain these documents, and indeed did not understand the importance of them.

After escrow closed the problems began to surface. The Buyers were not up to the management responsibilities, the maintenance was costly and unending, and the cash flow was not sufficient to cover the debt. The property was foreclosed and the Buyers lost everything. They sued their Agent and the broker, of course

Questions:
Is this clearly the Agent's fault? Well, you can guess that it is below the standard of care for the Agent to sell a 20-unit building with no prior experience or broker supervision. The issuance of a license through DRE gives Agents the right to sell any type of property anywhere in California. But should they? This lawsuit indicated

the Agent and broker were woefully below the knowledge level required to do this transaction.

What Agents Can Do:
There's a first time for everything. Agents may want to stretch their capabilities and handle unfamiliar transaction types. Agents can sell property outside of their familiar marketing area. This is not prohibited by the DRE nor by any ethical standards. The proper procedure when faced with a transaction beyond your normal capacities is to first check with your supervising broker to see if there is sufficient oversight to proceed. If not, consider referring the transaction to an Agent who can properly fulfill the standard of care. A referral fee is always better than a lawsuit.

Alternatively, engage the services of a licensee experienced in the type of transaction to assist you and make sure it is done properly. A small portion of the commission is an excellent insurance policy against a legal proceeding.

Finally, let your clients know that you are unfamiliar with the transaction type, or area. Let them know what steps you are taking to make sure they are properly represented. They will appreciate your honesty and your concerns for their best interests.

Postscript:
Does the Buyer in this case have any responsibility for their actions, or lack thereof? These Buyers acted foolishly by "signing off" on the overwhelming disclosure package, without reading or understanding it. They didn't ask questions. The law directs Buyers to look out for their own interests. The Buyers failed to do that, and had to take partial responsibility for their own losses. In the end, both parties to the lawsuit suffered losses of time, money, and reputation.

56. Do the Buyers Want you to Discriminate when Selecting their Home?

Use caution if the Buyers direct you to show them properties only in areas where there are no people of a particular race, color, religion, sex, national origin, marital status, handicap, or ancestry. If you follow their instructions, you may be guilty of steering. Such discriminatory practice is against both state and federal fair housing laws, as well as common sense. Agents who assist Buyers in doing so may find themselves drawn into costly and time-consuming litigation. Do the right thing. Advise Buyers to consider all homes based on the suitability and affordability of the home itself.

57. What if the Buyer Wants Specifics about Crime?

Buyers may inquire if there are any registered sex offenders in the community. Buyers may want to have the local crime statistics. This information is changeable from day to day. It is unwise for an Agent to provide such variable and fluctuating data, due to this changeability. The better procedure is for Buyers to make inquiries directly with the local police or sheriff departments, as well as seek information on websites that provide current statistics.

58. Buyer Asks "What Price Should I Offer?"

This question is a legitimate one coming from a Buyer. Buyers, after all, believe that Agents know values better than they do. Isn't that the Agent's job? However, use care when advising what price to offer, as this could be a land mine waiting to explode. If the Agent suggests an answer, what might happen?

If the suggested offered price is too low, the Buyer may lose out to a competitive bidder if there are other offers. Hopefully the Seller will make a counter offer price. This gives the Buyer the chance to stay in the competition. Although the Seller's counter offer may in fact be reasonable, the Buyer is now convinced that the original price suggested by the Agent was fair, otherwise why would the Agent have suggested it? The Buyer's Agent is in a tough spot. The Agent must go back to the Buyer and re-advise the higher price.

If the offered price is too high, and the Seller accepts the offer, the Buyer may feel they paid too much from the beginning. Buyer's remorse may set in.

What to do? Let the Buyer choose their offering price. It's not an Agent's job to determine the selling price of a property.

59. The Buyer Questions "Did I See Every Property?"

Once a suitable property has been targeted by the Buyer, the Agent should prepare an analysis of other similar properties which have been selling, or are presently available, in the area. This research may be called a Competitive Market Analysis or a Comparable Market Analysis. It may be computer-generated or completed by the Agent. Armed with this organized data, a Buyer can have a clearer grasp of what might be a reasonable offering price.

This market analysis also gives the Buyer the benefit to know what else is available, including any properties that may not have been shown to the Buyer. The Agent can have a discussion about why certain homes were eliminated, according to the Buyer's financial and other parameters. If the Buyer's criteria changed, the Agent can continue the search for a perfect match as the Buyer directs.

☞*Hint: Keep a copy of your prepared market analysis in the transaction file. This can help verify that the Buyer paid what was a reasonable market value at the time of sale.*

60. "Do You Think the Value Will Go Up?"

If Buyers believe they are getting a real bargain, they may expect the property to surely and swiftly rise in value. Where did they get that idea? If it came from you, look up and down the tracks to see the train headed for you. It's one thing for Buyers to think they are getting more than their money's worth, or that this purchase cannot lose. It's another for the Agent to assure them of this. No one can predict the future.

How can an enthusiastic Agent draw the line between sales puffery and real estate advice? It helps to consider the Agent's role as being a wise uncle or aunt advising the Buyer about the purchase. Agents have a fiduciary duty of utmost care, integrity, and loyalty. Point out whatever flaws and drawbacks you may observe as you enthuse about the property's positive aspects. Encourage Buyers to get all the information needed to make a decision that is right for them.

Writing an Offer

🖐 61.   Do the Buyers Seem Overwhelmed?

Have you ever counted the number of papers a Buyer signs during the average home purchase? Purchasing a property may be a daunting task for a Buyer. Finding a suitable home, making the right offer, reading and approving the mountain of paperwork, filling out piles of applications, etc. may leave a Buyer stressed out. Agents do real estate transactions regularly, after training and licensing. Agents are familiar with a huge assortment of forms. Most of it is routine, but all of it is important. If things go wrong, Buyers may claim that they were not given the paperwork, didn't understand it, or the Agent misrepresented what the Buyers signed.

Prevent this by carefully presenting each document, explaining its purpose, and taking the time to answer the Buyer's questions before they sign. Go over the paperwork when the Buyer is able to focus. Eliminate distractions where possible. If the Buyers have questions which involve a legal decision or interpretation, and the Agent is not acting as an attorney, recommend an attorney be consulted. Keep a record of what documents you discussed with the Buyer. When you deliver paperwork, have them initial and date in the appropriate sections.

Whenever possible, give the Buyer advance time to read over what is to be signed and ask questions, before the deadline for signatures. Nothing causes the brain to forget more quickly than being hurried!

☞ *Hint: It is usually an excellent practice to give the Buyer a blank copy of the sales agreement that is used in your area. They can look at it and ask questions before they have found their perfect property. They will be less stressed and better prepared to make the offer with you.*

🖐 62.   Will the Buyers be Making an All Cash Offer?

What's the problem with that? Nothing, except that an Agent should have some comfort level that the Buyer can deliver as represented. When the offer does not include a provision for the Buyer to secure a loan, advise the Buyers that they may have to produce financial assurances to the Seller once an offer is presented. Is the Buyer qualified to make such an offer? Agents do not have to be the private investigators of a Buyer's financial situation nor of amounts on deposit. Agents do have the duty to act with a reasonable level of skill when passing on a financial verification document…does it seem legitimate or bogus? Although the final approval of such documentation may rest with the Seller or the Seller's financial advisor, alert the parties if you find something amiss.

🖐 63.   Does the Buyer want to Purchase Property You Own?

Warning! Warning! Whom do you represent? At a minimum, you will have the burden and responsibilities of being both the Seller and the Seller's Agent. Don't get into the position of also representing the Buyer. Do you realize that if you are a licensee, you are considered to have superior knowledge to that of the general public? This is because you have a license, and the non-licensed consumer does not. You may represent yourself, but be certain to disavow any representation of the Buyer unless you like paying attorney's fees. It will help avoid claims that you took advantage of the unwary Buyer if the Buyer has his or her own real estate or legal representation.

✋ 64. What If the Buyer Wants to Make an
        Offer on Your Own Listing?

If so, this transaction will be dual agency, and dual licensee as well. This is allowed under California law, but may make the transaction much more difficult, as your fiduciary duties now apply to both parties. Some Agents feel their responsibilities under dual agency are compromised. You may not be the advocate for either the Seller or the Buyer. You are neutered, or I mean neutral, in the transaction. You cannot negotiate a better advantage for one against the other. Sort of takes the wind out of your sails, doesn't it?

If you don't want to be in this position, ask the Buyer to select someone to assist them as their Agent. If the Buyer selects a licensee within your real estate firm, it will still be dual agency but it will at least have the separation of two different licensees for the parties. If outside the real estate firm, there would be single and separate agency for both the Seller and Buyer.

Listing Agents who find themselves unwilling to handle a dual agency/dual licensee role have developed an alternative plan. They direct the Buyer to a short list of qualified and experienced Agents who are capable of representing Buyers in a single agency role. The Buyer makes his or her selection, and is referred to that Agent. Both Agents split the fee according to the procuring cause and work load. These Agents network with one another and other Agents who in turn refer dual agency/dual licensee situations back.

✋ 65. Is The Buyer a Real Estate licensee?

Whether in the home state or otherwise, it is advisable to note the Buyer's status as a licensee on the purchase agreement. A real estate license may introduce the concept of "superior knowledge" over the non-licensed Seller. Why take a chance that the Seller will later claim some unfair advantage that the Buyer had in the transaction?

66. Does the Buyer Plan to Fix-Up the Property and Resell?

There is nothing wrong with this plan. Hopefully the Buyer will make a big profit when the property is resold and all will be well. Of course, if the Seller feels that the sale was unfair and he or she should have been given the chance to make this profit, then you have to document the issues. To protect the Buyer against future claims by the Seller, keep a copy of the Competitive Market Analysis showing similar properties and what their sales prices were at the time. It can be difficult to go back several years and re-evaluate what a property was worth. Paperwork makes the situation much easier.

> ☞ *Hint: Agents may want to get the Seller's and Buyer's signatures or initials on their CMA to prove that they were provided with one.*

If the Buyer is a real estate licensee or a contractor, one extra step could be useful. If it is the Buyer's intention, state that the Buyer intends to fix up and re-sell the property at a profit in the transaction paperwork. Should the Seller have any objections to the Buyer's plan, it would be incumbent upon the Seller to speak up at the time the offer is negotiated. If the Seller thinks he or she is capable of doing the fix-up and selling for more, the Seller can select that course of action and keep the property. At least this disclosure will help protect the Buyer against future claims that the Buyer took "unfair advantage" of the Seller.

> ☞ *Hint: Advise the Buyer to go to the local planning department to find out what they can and cannot do with regard to renovations of the property.*

67. Is this a New Home Under Construction?

There are special purchase agreements for a newly constructed home or one which is to be completed prior to the transfer of title. Use them. These contracts address such issues as the occupancy permit, release of mechanics liens, plan changes and costs, and other concerns pertinent to a new home.

It is easy to have misunderstandings about the incomplete aspects of the home, such as floor finishes, light fixtures, color of paint, appliances, etc. Using the special contract for homes under construction encourages the Buyer and Seller/contractor to negotiate a "completion punch list" in writing between them. According to the level of completion, a Buyer may want to have an outside architect review the plans or blueprints to verify that the home is built as agreed. If the builder does not intend to give the plans to the Buyer, disclose this. It is common to find Buyers and builders making changes to the plans. If there are to be additional costs, these should be clearly identified and agreed between the parties. It may be advisable to have an attorney draw up these agreements.

There may be warranties on certain items or components of the house. Buyers and Sellers will want to understand what is covered and the limitations. Make sure all the appropriate warranties are delivered to the Buyer.

🖐 68.   Is This a New Home in a Subdivision?

Buyers will want to know what common area facilities (pool, tennis courts, etc.) are included and the expected completion date. Inform Buyers of special assessments or obligations to pay community facilities bonds (such as Mello-Roos), and the costs of these. Does the builder have the financial resources to finish the entire project? The Buyer may want to go onto the builder's website to check out the builder's history and background. Is the builder reputable? The local building department or business bureau may have a record of any complaints.

The California-mandated Real Estate Transfer Disclosure Statement (RETDS) may not be required of the builder if a subdivision report is used in its place. Be sure to obtain receipt of this. The Agent will still complete the Agent's Visual Inspection Disclosure (AVID).

In some cases, builders have their own purchase contract which is used. Agents will want to review this form and advise the Buyer to consult an attorney if there are any items of concern.

🖐 69.   The Home is New, so Why Bother with an Inspection?

Buyers may mistakenly believe that it isn't necessary for them to get inspections if the house is new. In fact, a new home may have more defects and pest infestation than a resale. After all, no one has yet lived in the home! Advise the Buyers accordingly.

70. What's an "As Is" Offer?

There's a lot of confusion about the "as is" clause or provision in a purchase agreement. When this clause is agreed to between the Seller and Buyer, it indicates that the Seller will not be responsible to the Buyers for the disclosed condition of the property, or to repair any property defects, whether known at the time of the offer or discovered later. Using this clause may cause confusion. One common misconception is that Sellers may think "as is" means they are not responsible to install or pay for any required government-mandated retrofit items such as smoke detectors, water heater bracing, etc. Not so!

Selling "as is" does not relieve Sellers from their duties to disclose any and all material facts. Using the term "as is" helps the Seller know that, at least for now, it is the Buyer's intention to take the property in its present condition, not come back to demand repair of these defects.

When there are multiple offers, it helps a Seller sort out those Buyers who are willing to go forward with the purchase in spite of the property's already-disclosed defects.

However, intentions are one thing and actualities are another. Certain protections for the Buyer of real estate give the Buyer an "out" if there are defects which were not disclosed. If these defects are not acceptable to the Buyer, the Buyer can withdraw from purchasing the property, or possibly make further negotiations with the Seller.

When the property is purchased "as is" and has items which are defects or red flags, two questions are important: 1) Were these defects disclosed to the Buyer before the offer was made or after? 2) Are all the defects known to the Seller and other parties fully disclosed?

Sellers cannot use the "as is" clause as a shield to hide or fail to disclose the property's problems. To do so would leave the Seller in a vulnerable position.

Disclosures for Buyers

🖐 71. The Buyers Already Know of the Defects, so Why Worry?

If a dispute arises at some future date, it will likely come from the Buyer claiming that a fact was not disclosed. If Buyers were informed, why don't they remember? Call it overwhelm, convenient memory, forgetfulness, or blame. Did the Buyers have the information they were supposed to receive? Can you prove it? For Agents, it's not just what you did, it's what you can prove you did. When you inform a Buyer about a defect, report, estimate, or other material fact, get your action documented in some way. Get a delivery receipt from the Buyer, make notes to your transaction log, send a cover letter or email, or note the presence of others. Be ready to prove you did your job.

☞ *Hint: Request the Seller give the Buyer copies of any inspections, reports, or estimates that may have been previously created. Even old reports can yield information that the Buyer is entitled to know.*

72. Is The Buyer Being Rushed to Complete the Sale?

It can be a huge problem if the Buyer is not given enough time to get any and all inspections the Buyer wants. Act in haste, repent at leisure. Sellers who think they are doing well to take an offer from a Buyer who waives inspections may want to think again. Undiscovered problems before title transfers may come back as deliberate attempts to cover up flaws.

If the reports generated on the property indicate "further inspections are recommended" give the Buyer enough time to decide how to proceed. It may be helpful to speak to the person who made the report and recommendation. If needed, have the Buyer seek out other inspectors or appropriate professionals. Agents will want to discuss the possible options and recommend that the Seller allow time for any additional inspections. This will help disclose any defects and better protect all the parties.

Advise a Buyer to read through the entire report. One lawsuit involved an inspection report that was 14 pages long. The Buyer signed a receipt for the report. After title transferred, many problems surfaced. At trial, it was discovered that only 4 pages of the report had actually been given to the Buyer.

☞ *Hint: When delivering or receipting a report, note the date of the report and the number of pages contained in the document.*

✋ 73.   If the Seller Won't Allow Inspections?

This is certainly a "red flag." Explore the reasons why the Seller is being uncooperative. It may be that the Seller has something to hide. This alone is a good reason to step back and take a second look at this transaction. If it is an issue of cost, a Buyer typically has the option of paying even if the Seller refuses. If it is a concern about disturbing the tenants, or perhaps the tenant makes the objection, a Buyer should think clearly about what baggage is coming with this property. Perhaps the Seller feels that the inspection will cause damage to the property. There may be ways to reassure or protect the Seller against any loss. Regardless of the situation, it should be clearly spelled out in writing. If the Buyer and Seller choose to waive a typically required inspection or right, obtain a legal opinion about how to proceed.

✋ 74.   Are there Special Disclosures for Common Interest Property?

There are quite a few important disclosures to consider. If the Buyer is purchasing a home, condo, or townhouse that is part of a common interest development (CID) community, there will likely be a Homeowner's Association (HOA) to which all property owners belong. The HOA sets the monthly fee paid by each property owner. This fee typically covers the cost of certain utilities, grounds and exterior maintenance, and a reserve amount for future expenses. There may also be costs for security, insurance, and other shared costs. If there are common-use facilities such as a pool, tennis court, tot lot, community house or similar, the HOA monthly dues may cover the property taxes and costs associated with them. Check the HOA dues carefully to see what is included in the monthly fee.

The HOA usually meets on a regular basis to discuss the budget and any items of interest to all owners. Meetings are typically conducted by a board of directors who are owners within the community. The HOA may set rules and regulations controlling the behavior of residents who live in the community. These can change from time to time. Ask if there is such a set of rules, and obtain them from the Seller if available.

Conditions and restrictions governing the appearance and use of properties within the community may also be in place and recorded as part of the title to the property. These are called Covenants, Conditions and Restrictions (CC&R's), and are available through the title company. Make sure the Buyer gets a full copy to read. Get a signed receipt when these are delivered to the Buyer.

> ☞ *Hint: Advise the Buyer to thoroughly read the CC&R's and all other HOA documents, as these affect the Buyer's use of the property. If the budget and reserve status is not clear to the Buyer, suggest they have an independent business or financial advisor look over the documents.*

The Seller will have to produce other documents pertinent to the HOA so the Buyer can review and approve them (see red flag items 29 and 30). These additional documents include but are not limited to the current Rules and Regulations, minutes of prior HOA meetings, and reserve and budget projections. If there are transfer fees or deposits required of the potential Buyer, the HOA documents should be able to provide this information.

> ☞ *Hint: The Homeowner's Association may offer a "field inspection" to verify that the property exterior is in compliance with current CC&R's.*

When the Buyer wants to Purchase a Home that's a Short Sale

✋ 75.   Is a Short Sale a Problem for Buyers?

Yes, it can be, due to several issues. Basically, a short sale occurs when the Buyer's offered price is not enough to pay off the Seller's loans, liens, and costs to sell the property. The short sale procedure is that the Buyer makes a written offer, the Seller negotiates what will be acceptable, and both parties eventually sign a purchase contract. Now the total amount of debt against the property must be addressed, or the sale cannot proceed. The Seller's next step is to gain approval of the Lender(s) to reduce the amount of the payoff demand so that a sale can take place. There is no guarantee that the Lender will take less than what is owed. Some Lenders prefer to foreclose.

It typically takes a lot of time for Lenders to respond to the short sale offer, once the Seller has accepted it. The Seller, and Agent, typically must provide a mountain of paperwork to justify their request that the debt be reduced. It is difficult to predict how much time this substantial paperwork can take, as Lenders vary according to their staffing, location, and number of loans being serviced. The Buyer may want to wait until a Lender gives approval of the sales contract, before spending money on inspections and reports. In addition, Buyers who pay loan origination fees will want to work with their Agent and new Lender to minimize non-refundable upfront costs.

In some cases, Lenders who agree to a reduction in the loan payoff have placed written conditions on their approval. Lenders may require that the Seller agree to a future payment, a deferred lien. Lenders have also been known to require that the Seller submit any other offers received in case there is a higher offer which could yield more money to the Lender. This Lender requirement has caused a great deal of friction, since neither Buyer nor Seller want to start over. In these situations, the Seller's Agent must comply with the Lender's requirements or risk violating the reduction in payoff offered by the Lender.

✋ 76. Why Use a Short Sale Addendum?

As previously discussed, the Seller faced with a short sale may have no control over whether the sale will go forward or not. If an offer from a Buyer will not cover the Seller's liens, the Lender or lien holders must decide what they will do. The Seller's acceptance of the Buyer's offer would be contingent upon the Lender's approval. Agents should include a Short Sale Addendum to inform the Buyer about the uncertainties and considerations. This might include:

✓ The offer is contingent upon the approval of the Lenders.

✓ The offer is contingent upon the Lenders reducing the amount of the debt owed by the Seller.

✓ Buyers may not want to spend money on inspections or loan commitments until they are certain that the sale can take place.

✓ The offer is contingent upon release of the Seller's debts.

✓ This process may take a lot of time.

Agents are typically able to advise the Lender about the current market prices and economic factors, such as the condition of the property and how long properties are taking to sell. Lenders evaluate the Seller's other assets and the likely costs if they choose to foreclose. With such information, Lenders can make a decision whether to accept less than the amount owed them or consider other alternatives.

☞Hint: Once the Lenders agree to take a reduction in the payoff, and the Seller has no further objections to the Lender's terms, the Buyer can be notified and time periods for the parties to perform their obligations can begin.

When the Listing is in Foreclosure

🖐 77.   What Constitutes the Foreclosure Process?

When a Lender or lien holder takes possession of a property pledged to satisfy a debt, the property is foreclosed. In California, the foreclosure process starts when a Notice of Default is filed (recorded) against the property. It is recorded in the county where the property is located. This notice of delinquent debt is generated by the lien holder or Lender. Once this occurs, the property is said to "be in foreclosure."

The foreclosure time frame takes several months to complete. During this period, offers received are presented to the Seller. It is advisable to keep the foreclosing Lenders informed of the current situation. The Seller typically has several opportunities to remove or stall the foreclosure. If the Lender knows what's going on, it may encourage cooperation, which is usually beneficial to all concerned.

> ☞ *Hint: Agents working with a property in foreclosure will want to consider that the Seller may be distressed and anxious to encourage a sale. The Seller may not be forthcoming about the property's defects. Sellers in foreclosure may feel they have little to lose if they fail to disclose everything. Advise the Buyers to get full inspections of the property and not rely on the Seller's representations alone.*

78. Is the Buyer an Investor? There May be Special Requirements.

The rules are different when the Buyer of an owner-occupied home (one-to-four units is included) does not intend to live in the property. In California, a special sales agreement must be used. This contract spells out the Seller's right to rescind the transaction. This provision is intended to safeguard distressed property homeowners from unscrupulous Buyers.

In addition, Agents must provide a Declaration of Proof of License. This signed statement provides the Agent's Department of Real Estate license number and is required in this contract between the homeowner/Seller and the investor/Buyer.

Red Flags when Drafting the Offer

🖐 79.   Did the Agents Draw up a Waiver?

A licensee's duty includes filling in the blanks of the sales agreements and other documents pertinent to a real estate transaction. Agents generate and memorialize agreements between the parties, as oral statements may be disputed and unenforceable. There seem to be pre-printed documents for every aspect of a real estate transaction. It is folly for Agents to be drafting their own documents, unless they are the attorneys in the transaction.

If Agents create documents that are ambiguous, that is, confusing in their purpose or terms, such a document is construed *against* the person who created the ambiguity. Avoid being the target…let attorneys draw up complex documents.

Of particular concern are documents which purport to waive any rights of the parties involved. Such waivers may or may not violate existing law. Clients should be referred to their respective legal counsel for opinion and drafting of these waivers. If necessary, allow additional time for the parties to consult with the appropriate advisor.

☞ *Hint: If you write it, you own it!*

✋ 80. What's the Difference Between a Contingency and a Covenant?

Real estate purchase contracts are considered legal, binding agreements between the Seller and Buyer. Agents should be extremely careful if they start creating Addenda or Exhibits to the standard contracts with the intent to spell out further obligations of either Buyer of Seller. When signed, the parties may have obligated themselves to perform some task they didn't intend to do.

The typical purchase contract contains several contingencies. If one party doesn't have to do anything unless they approve of further information or until after the other party does something, this is a contingency. It's similar to saying "I'll do this *if and when* you do that." Another way to think of a contingency is "I'll do this only *if and when* I approve of what I get."

If the party is agreeing to do the task *without fail*, this may be a covenant or promise. This is similar to saying "I'll do this, regardless." There is a big difference between a contingency and a covenant. Agents who draft documents run the risk of misstating the intentions of their principals. Get supervisory or legal counsel on what you want to say. Who want to be on the firing line?

✋ 81.   Should you Advise Litigation or Arbitration?

Neither. California agreements typically provide an option for the parties to pre-select whether they will settle future disputes through litigation or arbitration. Most Agents can explain that litigation involves filing a lawsuit and a decision by a judge or jury. Arbitration is considered an alternative dispute resolution done outside of court, and decisions are rendered through one or more arbitrators. There's much more to it, of course. Each method to settle disputes has its benefits and drawbacks.

Agents should not attempt to explain the legal ramifications of either method, nor should they advise their clients which method to choose. There are many important considerations and rights involved. Refer questions like "Which one do you advise?" or "What do most people select?" to the client's legal advisor.

82. Should the Buyer Select Liquidated Damages or Not?

California purchase agreements provide the liquidated damages option to allow Buyers to pre-limit the extent of their "damages," or payment to the Seller should the Buyers default in the purchase. The contract paragraph specifies that this agreement applies only if the property is one-to-four residential units and the Buyer intends to occupy one of the units as a principal residence. In the case of a Buyer's default, the Seller may be entitled to keep the Buyer's deposit amount up to the maximum specified. The liquidated damages amount does not automatically go to the Seller, as a Buyer default must be acknowledged or proven.

The amount, if pre-agreed, is stated in the contract as limited to 3% of the home's purchase price. This amount may actually be less, if the Buyer's total deposits are less than this amount. The amount of liquidated damages may, on occasion, be changed with the counsel of an attorney. Agents should be willing to explain the purpose of this liquidated damages provision, but should not advise whether to decline, change this amount or select it. The Buyer's decision is appropriately initialed in the purchase agreement.

Since the Buyer is the one making the initial offer to purchase, the Buyer states his or her preference. The Seller will need to agree to the Buyer's request, counter the offer's provision, or decline to accept the offer. Both parties will have to agree on this issue before the contract can be considered ratified, or binding.

83. Is the Buyer Increasing the Initial Deposit?

Did the Buyer and Seller agree to and initial the liquidated damages provision in the purchase agreement? If so, any increase in the Buyer's deposit may be intended as part of the liquidated damages. Read the agreement between the parties. If appropriate, secure the appropriate paperwork signed by the Buyer to include this deposit in the liquidated damages provision. If this additional paperwork is not signed, the increased deposit may not be considered as part of the liquidated damages amount.

84. What about Paperwork - Can the Agent
   Deliver, Receipt, or Accept?

That depends. What does the purchase agreement state? There is a difference between delivering a document and having it accepted or receipted, as real estate attorneys will tell you. If you FAX a document, you may have delivered it, but is it accepted? What about constructive receipt? Attorneys can argue about these concepts for hours. Don't get yourself in a position of litigating and interpreting "who did what". Just read the contract and follow the rules as specified. To do otherwise puts the client at risk.

Hint: Watch those time frames! If your client cannot perform by the date specified, make your client's intentions known in writing. Follow the specified timing to advise your client to perform, remove contingencies, or decline to do so. Request extensions when appropriate and get signed approval from all parties.

85. "Can't You Just Sign it for Me?"

Oh, no, don't! Unless you have their power of attorney (and that may cause issues as well), Agents should neither sign nor initial for their clients. Too much litigation has resulted from this. Considering how mobile our society is today, it should be easy to get in touch with clients by FAX, email, or overnight courier. There is no such thing as a "routine form that needs your approval." The form may be standard, but if a signature or initial is required, it must be significant.

> ☞ *Hint: Give your clients enough time to read and review the paperwork they are being given. Avoid the tendency to stack up the documents and say, "Just begin initialing at the top and work your way down the pile." Make it your practice to review the documents requiring signatures. Save yourself a lot of grief. Sit down with your clients while they wade through the paperwork.*

86. So Many Counter Offers – What Did We End up With Anyway?

The offer goes back and forth, forth and back, proposals and counter-proposals, addendum #1, #2, #3. By the time the Agents believe that the Buyer and Seller have reached an agreement, it could be difficult to know what is final. Agents should read all the subsequent modifications to make sure they reference back to the original sales contract. Do the documents make sense when they are all put together?

In some instances, if all the parties agree, it may make sense to re-write the sales agreement to cleanly and clearly capture all the intents of the parties.

87. When Does the Buyer Get Back the Deposit?

When an offer fails to go forward, the return of the Buyer's deposit should be timely. The Buyer's Agent can return the deposit at any time if the offer was never ratified or accepted by the Seller, and there was no contract. The Buyer may also request the check be returned if the offer has not yet been presented.

In either case, the Agent will want written documentation that the check was returned to the Buyer. This can be accomplished by a cover letter with the voided or shredded check, or personal delivery with a receipt. Under trust fund regulations, the Agent is responsible for the Buyer's check.

It takes a bit longer to accomplish the return of a Buyer's deposit if the transaction was begun but was not completed, that is, escrow was opened using the Buyer's check. The escrow holder of the funds will issue a refund check as specified by the parties. The escrow company, acting in a neutral capacity, will want to have the approval of both Seller and Buyer, and the real estate firms, before returning the deposit. If there were costs incurred by the Buyer, these may be deducted. If the Seller has a dispute about the return of the Buyer's deposit, and withholds approval, it may cause delays. California law provides a fine of up to $1000 against a Seller who withholds approval to return a Buyer's deposit when no "good faith dispute" exists.

🗁 In a Slow Market, How Low Can You Go?

What price should the Buyers offer? Let us assume for this discussion that the real estate market is slow at present. Homes take a while to sell, and there is a lot of inventory from which Buyers can choose. Buyers are taking their time to shop, and shop some more. Sellers are anxious to see an offer on their properties. When Buyers find a suitable home, Agents encourage Buyers to make an offer, based upon other sales data and the Buyers' own preferences. But how low can a Buyer go? Is there a formula for determining the percentage off the asking price?

No. There is no rule of thumb you can apply to all listings. The asking prices and showing conditions differ from area to area, and from price range to price range. Very similar properties have incredibly different asking prices. The reasons may include the motivation of Sellers, specific amenities which are difficult to value, helpful financing, uniqueness of the home, or possibly Agents lacking the knowledge to correctly price their listings. As a result, the asking price on the property could be either high for the current market, or it might be priced just where it should be, or lower. If it's high, Buyers might make an offer anywhere less than the asking price. If the asking price is correct for the market, multiple Buyers may make offers.

If the home is perceived to be priced under the market value, Buyers may be surprised to see that there are multiple offers, and perhaps even a bidding war. This can occur in all areas, with all types of properties. A Buyer's low offer may not stand up to this competition. Advise Buyers of the facts. Let them know what comparable properties are selling for. Buyers in a slow market may have been reading newspaper articles which tell them that "all" homes will take a low offer or sell for less than asking. Not necessarily so!

Sellers have the same information about recent sales and current listings as you do. Any competent listing Agent will make sure of this when an offer is presented. Inform Buyers about the market to help them come up with a price that will be a good deal for them, yet acceptable to the Sellers.

As a Buyer's Agent, don't suggest the price for your clients to offer. Your job is to do the research to help the Buyers decide what offer to make. First, check out what comparable properties have sold very recently, and for what price they sold. Make sure they are similar in size, location, and style to the home your Buyers want to buy. Don't consider any sales which closed more than 60 days ago, if possible, to make sure you are reflecting the current market conditions.

Take a look at what's on the market now, and their asking prices. Go shopping, as Buyers will want to check out all their options. Is there a big difference between the asking prices and the actual sold prices? This indicates that the market is dropping. You can encourage Buyers to bring in an offer that is below the asking price, as long as it matches the range of "sold and closed" prices.

Why bother hitting the target range? Why not just make an offer, no matter how low, and see how the Seller responds? Many Agents think this is a good strategy, but this plan often backfires. If the Buyers' offer is way off the mark, Sellers may be insulted and angry, and may choose not to even counter the offer. Some Sellers have the reaction "Is this Buyer serious? I don't want to give away my home."

When you advise your Buyers to hit the target range, and the offer is close to reality, the Seller can feel compelled to take the offer, even if it is lower than what they wanted. If your price is "out of range" and unreasonably low, you may get a counter offer at nearly the Seller's asking price. Sellers may decide to not even trouble themselves with a counter offer. They may dismiss an offer that is too low. Sellers have no obligation to give Buyers a response.

Here's a better strategy: A sale typically includes two negotiations: one is the price offered, and the second is the negotiation during the discovery period. This is when the repairs and defects are negotiated. Once your offer is accepted, and you are in escrow, the Sellers and Buyers may be highly motivated to negotiate the cost of any items which show up on the inspections. If you have your sale in escrow, Sellers may be relieved that their home is about to be sold. Most Sellers will be reluctant to blow their sale out of the water over Buyers' subsequent requests. You may not want to negotiate all the potential repair costs at the time you present the offer. Leave the door open for whatever costs you find later. The Seller may be inclined to keep the escrow going, and Buyers may be of a similar mind, otherwise the Buyers have to begin their search anew. Neither party wants to face the option of starting over.

SECTION III:
MOVING THE SALE THROUGH TO CLOSING

The Escrow Process

88. One Party Wants to Delay Opening Escrow

The escrow holder serves in a neutral capacity, acting upon the written instructions of the parties to the transaction. The Buyer's deposit is typically delivered to the escrow company along with details of the transaction. These details will include sale price, Seller credits, name and information about the Buyer and Seller, expected date to transfer title, etc. If one party wishes to hold off on beginning this process, the Agent needs to determine the reason behind the reluctance. Uncover issues before they become problems. Inform both parties what to expect.

DON'T SHOOT ME... I'M JUST THE REAL ESTATE AGENT!

📁Did Anyone Read the Preliminary Title Report (PTR)?

In this lawsuit, the Buyer made an offer on a house, contingent upon him selling his present home. The Sellers responded "no contingency offers" so the Buyer wrote up another offer without one. Sellers accepted and escrow was opened. Buyer was notified of acceptance and put his home on the market immediately. He didn't want to make payments on two homes.

The Sellers advised their Agent in confidence that they owed money to the IRS and had a few other court-ordered settlements on record against them. The Sellers asked their Agent to hold off delivering the Preliminary Title Report (PTR) to the Buyer so they might clear these debts from the title report. The Agent, a dual agent who was also representing the Buyer, agreed to wait a few weeks before showing the PTR to the Buyer. The Buyer was unaware of any of this and was assured the transaction was proceeding as planned.

The Buyer's home sold. A few days away from closing escrow on the Buyer's home, the Buyer asked about the missing PTR on his new home. With one glance at the PTR, it was clear that the Sellers were not able to remove the money judgments on title, and there was insufficient equity to pay these liens. The Buyer was compelled to complete the sale on his present residence, but had no home to move into. Left homeless, he consulted an attorney.

Advisory:
The Agent's fiduciary duties of utmost care, integrity, honesty and loyalty to a client are clear. A licensee is also expected to be knowledgeable in real estate matters. The Preliminary Title Report, or PTR, is a snapshot of the recorded liens, easements, and other matters of records which affect the property.

The delivery of the PTR to the Buyer is typically called for in the purchase contract. It is an Agent's duty to take a look at the PTR to question any potential problems. An Agent should call any such issues to the client's attention. In this case, the seriousness of the Seller's liens overburdening the property raised a red flag. This should have been disclosed to the Buyer. Even though the Seller's debts are a confidential matter, if such debts will prevent escrow from closing, or delay the close, it is a material fact affecting the value or desirability of the property.

There are lesser issues of title which can be a red flag to the Buyers. As an example, if the Buyer indicates an intention to put a pool in the back yard, and the PTR shows an easement for an underground utility pipe in the area, the problem is obvious. Some title issues can be resolved with enough time (see red flag #4, 5, 6). Some cannot be resolved.

In many cases the PTR indicates the existence of another document by recorded reference to it. The presence of a lease may be indicated by a recorded memorandum. Covenants, Conditions, and Restrictions (CC&R's) are typically indicated by reference. Agents should ask the title company for a copy of such further documents.

Summary Points:
Is an Agent required to interpret the PTR? No. If the Agent or client has questions, the appropriate title officer should be contacted for answers. Put your client in touch with the title officer. If you relay such information, be sure to quote your source and whether you have verified it or not.

Is the PTR accurate? No. That's why it's called, "Preliminary Title Report". It is an offer from the Title Company to issue a policy of title insurance. These reports are updated every few weeks, so the PTR you get today might have been run last month. Yesterday's new lien may not show up at all. It is also true that a recorded Deed of Trust reflects the original amount of the Note, not necessarily the current balance.

Should Agents advise the Buyers to read the PTR? Yes. Buyers may not be aware that the matters of title, which are on record, can and do impact their ability to use and enjoy the property. This same standard of care applies to Agents who sell properties that have Covenants, Conditions, and Restrictions (CC&R's) recorded. One Agent carelessly told his Buyers to "read these CC&R's only when you want to fall asleep" and was sued for this poor advice. Agents should let their clients know how important it is to read what they *can* and *cannot* do with the property they are buying.

✋ 89.   Did the Buyer's Deposit Check Bounce?

Uh oh! This is a problem, and Sellers' Agents need to inform their clients about this development. Keep Sellers fully apprised if this situation occurs. The solution may be easy and quick. Or the solution may be painful and dragged out. If the shortage cannot be corrected, seek a legal opinion of how to proceed.

✋ 90.   Doesn't Canceling the Escrow Cancel the Purchase Agreement?

When a sale does not go forward, the parties typically must sign cancellation of escrow instructions in order for the return of deposits to be made by the escrow holder. Agents may mistakenly believe that cancellation of the escrow and return of appropriate deposits cancels the sale. Not so. The purchase agreement, ratified between the principals, is a legal document and may still be in effect. It is necessary to have the parties agree that the existing contract is null and void. This should be done in writing and signed by the parties. This may help protect a Seller who wishes to resell the property to a new Buyer, and help protect a Buyer who wants to move on to another property.

Agents may cancel an escrow and open escrow with another company if the situation is in the principals' best interests. Of course, the principals must agree to this plan and sign the appropriate paperwork.

> ☞ Hint: Agents should advise the Seller that all reports, inspections, appraisals, and estimates which were obtained will need to be disclosed to the next Buyer.

✋ 91.   Which Agent is Ordering What Reports?

The purchase agreement may specify that inspections, home warranties, reports, and the like are to be provided. Does the contract call for a home warranty? Who is responsible for securing these? Communicate with the other Agent and decide who does what. Work as a team to get the transaction fulfilled according to the instructions of the Buyers and Sellers. Don't let the time frames run out, as this may be trouble for both Agents.

92. Why is Insurance Not so Easy Anymore?

Insurance companies have suffered major losses from a variety of natural catastrophes. New insurance fraud schemes pop up daily. As a result, companies have increased their requirements and decreased their coverage. Some insurance firms decline to offer coverage in certain geographic areas, or charge higher rates from one area to another. Insurance companies may also run a report to check out the claims that were filed against the home by the current owner. Prior water intrusion claims may make a new policy difficult or costly if the insurance company thinks the problem has not been solved. Insurance companies may be restrictive about writing homeowner's policies to unknown (new) customers. Buyers will have to shop for coverage and rates that are acceptable.

Lenders typically have requirements that a Buyer provide an insurance policy prior to title transferring. The Lender will specify their requirements for fire and liability coverage. Lenders may also require flood insurance, according to the property's location. The lack of a readily available insurance policy may delay, or even prevent, the sale from being completed. Advise the Buyer of the market conditions, and suggest that the Buyer get started on acquiring an insurance policy as soon as the escrow is opened. Time can yield better results than pressure.

> ☞ *Hint: Renters starting the search for their first home purchase may find it helpful to purchase a "renter's contents policy" with an established insurance company. Such inexpensive policies are easily obtained and can be converted to a homeowner's policy when the home search is successful. With such a policy, the renter is not considered a "new customer" to the insurance company!*

☝ 93. Is there Income from Rental Property?

If the property has income, the Buyer will want documentation of the specifics. In addition to the rental income, the Buyer will want to know the property expenses, deferred maintenance items, maintenance contracts, legal costs, etc. What personal property comes with the purchase, and which items belong to the tenants? Is any of the equipment leased, like the laundry facilities or vending machines?

The Seller may be asked to complete an Affidavit verifying the rents and deposits. The tenants may be asked for estoppels, as discussed earlier. Estoppels verify the rent, deposits, and any claims or offsets to the rental agreement and are signed by the tenants. Lenders may have their own estoppels which they require as a condition of granting the loan. Ask for them well in advance, as it may take time for the Agent to obtain the tenants' signatures and deliver to the Lender.

Deliver copies of the existing leases or rental agreements to escrow or directly to the Buyer and receipt these.

> ☞ *Hint: If the tenant security deposits are transferred to the Buyer, the Seller will want to make sure that the existing tenants are legally notified that their deposits now rest with the new owner. If this is not done, the former owner may find themselves responsible for returning deposits to tenants when they vacate.*

94. Is the Seller Crediting Funds to the Buyer?

This is not necessarily a problem, as long as the amount does not exceed the non-recurring closing costs. Sellers may choose to pay some or all of Buyer's typical costs to complete the sale. Generally, the Lender may not approve if the Seller is perceived as making a contribution to the Buyer's down payment. This may violate the Lender's underwriting guidelines. Check with the Buyer's Lender. Sellers are generally permitted to pay for the Buyer's appraisal, title insurance, loan points, escrow fees, notary and document fees, HOA transfer charges, and the like. Sellers generally may not pay for the Buyer's property insurance, property taxes, HOA dues, etc. as these costs are continuing.

95. Does the Buyer Have a Home to Sell?

Coordinating two closings can be difficult. If the Buyer is also the Seller on an existing home, allow time for extensions. You'll probably need them. The Buyer may need funds from the sale of an existing property in order to close on the next property. Is the successful closing on the Buyer's existing property a contingency? Will the Seller be cooperative if more time is needed? Discuss these scenarios at the time the offer is made, and obtain the Seller's agreement to extend the time frame if it proves necessary.

Getting Signatures on Documents

✋ 96. Are the Parties Out of Town?

If so, the Buyer or Seller may not be present for the actual signing of documents. Agents should discuss the situation in advance to determine the best solution. Escrow can prepare most documents ahead of schedule if requested. Lenders may find it difficult to do this, however they may be flexible if given enough lead time.

✋ 97. Is there a Power of Attorney?

The Power of Attorney gives one party the right to act and sign documents for another. The party giving authority to another is the principal. The person acting for the principal is referred to as their attorney-in-fact. Although it may sound confusing, an attorney-in-fact does not have to be an attorney at all.

A power of attorney may be appropriate if a principal is, or plans to be, out-of-town or unavailable when the principal's signatures are required.

There are two types of powers of attorney. A specific power of attorney gives the attorney-in-fact the right to act for their principal in a specific function or for a specific purpose. A general power of attorney gives the attorney-in-fact greater abilities and may not be limited to a single task.

Real estate paperwork may be signed by a principal's attorney-in-fact. Agents should be cautious when someone purports to have a power of attorney. Ask to see it. Whenever possible, meet with the principal to reassure yourself that the power of attorney has been freely given.

Have the original power of attorney document approved by the escrow company or a legal advisor to determine that it was done correctly. Is it appropriate to the task at hand? Is it current? Will the Lender allow the power of attorney to be used in any of the loan documents, if necessary?

Typically, real estate title documents including grant deeds are notarized before they are recorded. Does the power of attorney give authority to transfer title? If so, the original power of attorney is usually notarized and recorded before a title company will be willing to insure the title.

98. Does the Offer Indicate an "Assignee"?

If so, who will actually be buying the property? Who will be fulfilling the terms of the contract? It can be a red flag if the true Buyer is not made clear to the parties. Does the Buyer intend to resell the property in escrow? Does the Buyer intend to bring in partners? Is the offer contingent upon finding an assignee? Ask questions to be sure that this transaction is going forward as indicated.

📁Who is the Actually the Buyer?

Quick glimpse of this case:
A Buyer made an offer that included the right to assign the purchase agreement. Using the phrase "or assignee" indicated that the Buyer in this transaction was acting in the role of a "scout" for other Buyers. The strategy was for the scout to tie up the property and then finds a replacement Buyer, with the intent of making a profit or a partnership purchase. No problem so far.

This contract between the Seller and the scout was ratified and escrow was opened. Shortly thereafter, the scout found a replacement Buyer for the property. The scout turned over his purchase rights to this Buyer, but never did so with any formal agreement. There was no assignment of the contract. The scout simply substituted the Buyer's name into all disclosure documents and removals of contingencies.

The Agent, who had written up the agreement and started the transaction and escrow with the scout, soon knew there was to be a different Buyer taking title. The Agent, however, continued to deliver disclosures and contingency removals to the scout. The scout forwarded these documents to the assignee Buyer. This Buyer, relying on the scout, initialed and signed as instructed. The Agent had no contact with the Buyer at all, conducting business only with the scout.

Now it gets really interesting:
Based on repairs discovered, the purchase price was re-negotiated and lowered during the escrow. Rather than use an Addendum, the Agent redrafted page one of the purchase agreement to reflect the negotiated price. The Agent took off the scout's name and put the Buyer's name into the paperwork. Buyer signed. Seller re-signed with the new Buyer and escrow continued. The agency relationship paragraph confirmed the Agent now represented the

newly-named Buyer. Keep in mind that the Buyer, not the scout, signed this contract. The Buyer still had no contact with the Agent, relying totally upon the scout for advice and assistance.

The Buyer closed escrow, and took title. When later problems surfaced between the Buyer and the scout, the Agent was brought into the litigation. The Agent protested "I never met this Buyer, I never sent them anything, and I don't know anything about them, so I don't represent them. I only represented the scout Buyer." Would you agree with this defense?

Advisory:
The problems started when the Agent filled in the "confirmation of agency" paragraph, indicating the fiduciary duty to represent the Buyer. The Agent never met the actual Buyer, never sent them documents, and knew nothing about them except their names. Agency Law is clear that our duties of "utmost care, integrity, honesty, and loyalty" exist once agency is created. Can we do this if we never have contact with the client? Are we obligated to represent clients we have never met? *And if we never have any contact, how could agency be created?*

In fact, this transaction demonstrates how paperwork created the agency, not the actions of the Agent or client. The fiduciary duties existed from Agent to Buyer, even though there was no client contact. When the client suffered damages, the Agent was implicated.

Summary:
This Agent did nothing to represent the Buyer, even though the Agent's name was confirmed on the agency line. The Agent was unable to show there was any care, integrity, honesty, or loyalty given to the Buyer. The Agent paid dearly for this mistake. The Agent was bound to be the fiduciary once the purchase agreement was signed with the Agent confirmation with the named Buyer, not the scout.

Yes, you can be involved in a transaction without creating agency, but you must be careful about your words and actions, as well as disavow any agency relationship in the paperwork. If "no agency" is your goal, be very clear.

If your contract allows the Buyer to substitute an assignee, it's advisable to use a written assignment, or a substitution of contract if all parties agree. Your escrow holder needs to be involved. Get a legal opinion to make sure it's done properly.

✋ 99. Can Documents be Notarized Out of State?

In California, real estate transfer documents are typically recorded in the county where the property is located. Prior to recordation, the signatures on these documents are notarized by a Notary Public licensed by the state. The purpose of notarization is to help prevent signatures from being forged. Notarizing a signature can take many forms.

The most common circumstance is where the signing party typically appears, is satisfactorily identified by the Notary, acknowledges his or her signature, and signs the Notary's journal, including a fingerprint. Note that there are special types of notarizations where the signing party does not have to personally appear. Once satisfied the signature is valid, the Notary then stamps the document and dates and signs as witness. A notary can also affix the proper stamped-and-signed form to the document being signed.

The "personal appearance" part of this process can be difficult if the principal is out-of-town, or out of the country. Usually, but not always, an out-of-state Notary Public can notarize the documents to be recorded in California. It is also possible to have documents notarized in a foreign country. If this situation is anticipated, find out if the party requesting the notarization will be satisfied if it is done out-of-state. Get the documents notarized early so the local county recorder's office can approve of the out-of-state notarization. If there is a problem, it can be solved. It just will take time.

☞ *Hint: A notarized signature is merely one level of assurance that the signature is valid, according to the Notary Public who stamped the document. It is not a guarantee! The document may still be a forgery.*

The Finish Line Details

✋ 100. Can the Buyer Write a Check to Transfer Title?

It is standard practice that escrow companies have "good funds" the day before escrow is expected to record the transfer of title. Most escrow companies prefer the funds be wired to them to assure the funds are legitimate. There may be instances where the funds are deposited the same day as the transfer, although these are special situations and arrangements are usually made in advance.

The Buyer may want to write a check to the escrow company for the balance of funds needed to complete the sale. Unfortunately, escrow companies may not be willing to allow this unless there is sufficient time for the funds to clear. Many banking institutions place a "hold" on large funds if deposited by check. Checks drawn from money market funds may also be restricted by a time requirement for funds to be liquidated. Even a cashier's check may be at odds with an escrow company's requirements.

Agents will want to discuss the source of the balance of the down payment and closing costs with the Buyer. Find out your escrow company's rules, and relay this information to the Buyer. Discuss the transfer and deposit of funds with the Buyer, how the funds will be deposited to escrow, and avoid a last-minute panic.

> ☞ *Hint: If you represent a Buyer, try to arrange that the escrow does not close on a Monday, or a Tuesday following a legal holiday. Why? Since the funds from the Lender must be deposited into escrow the business day before the closing, if the closing is on Monday, the funds are deposited the prior Friday. The Buyer pays interest on the new loan as of the date the funds go into escrow, and will end up paying interest for the loan on Friday, Saturday, and Sunday — three days of interest for nothing! Close on Tuesday (or the rest of the week), pay interest only for one day, and be the Buyer's hero! You're welcome!*

POSTSCRIPT

What is giving rise to so many lawsuits today?

It may be that real estate has lost value, or didn't make the profit the owner expected. It might be that property owners find themselves in distressed situations. Perhaps the property has costly flaws that were discovered after the Buyer purchased.

Whatever the reason, it's tempting to want to blame someone. The real estate Agents and their companies make good targets. After all, the real estate Agents are licensed. They've sold other properties. They should know what to do. Since things went wrong, didn't the Agents and their actions contribute to these problems?

Many times the public's perception of an Agent's duty is greater than the actual job description. Buyers and Sellers may not fully understand what real estate Agents do and don't do. Unless a licensee can clarify where their duties start and stop, this may lead to erroneous assumptions. Assumptions often become problems.

Each of the 100 transactions contained in this book was drawn from recent litigation. Only cases that actually went to trial are in the public record. 90% of real estate cases settled out of court, and are NOT known to most real estate Agents.

I am not an attorney and this book does not purport to give legal advice. The recommendations are based on current standards of behavior for California real estate licensees as of the date of publication. *Things change.* Do not consider the advice or issues contained in this book to be the "final word" on the duties or responsibilities of licensees. They are not.

Whether you are a Seller, Buyer, or Agent, I thank you for selecting this book to be a resource for you. Since we all know our industry is constantly evolving, I will attempt to keep this book's information updated on my website: www.TopRealEstateRisk.com.

If you are an Agent, please alert me to changes in practices and situations as they occur in your area. Let me know if you have another great suggestion to solve any of these red flags, too. I'd appreciate it!

Hopefully these examples will help Buyers, Sellers, and you, the Agent, complete each transaction with fully satisfying results. Beware of the red flags, manage the risks, and continued success to you!

ABOUT THE AUTHOR

Cari Lynn Pace is a California broker licensed since 1974. She has sold, leased, and managed just about every type of property, both residential and commercial. She's authored dozens of professional articles, Agent training seminars, and courses accredited by the California Department of Real Estate. Cari wrote two training books for the REBS division of the California Association of Realtors®, and is the editor of LawsuitPreventionServices.blogspot.com. She continues to serve as an advisor and expert witness for many attorneys in Northern California. Cari earned five national designations (GRI, CCIM, CRB, CRS, CCDC) and was elected as President of the Marin Association of Realtors®, where she was recently awarded their Distinguished Service Award recognizing years of outstanding service to the real estate industry and to the community.

Cari clearly loves sharing her experiences through teaching and speaking engagements and can be reached via email at TopRealEstateRisk@gmail.com or through her website www.TopRealEstateRisk.com. She and her husband Bob Koch, a retired physician, live in Marin County, Ca.

Since Cari's daughter Katie and her son Rob are away at college, she would probably enjoy traveling to your group to deliver a keynote speech or workshop. Cari is also available for consultation on real estate disputes. You may reach Cari through her website at www.TopRealEstateRisk.com or by emailing her at TopRealEstateRisk@gmail.com. In California, her phone number is (415) 893-9888.